The Career Direc...
The Internships Series

The two most-praised series of career books ever published, each has been named "Best of the Best" by the American Library Association:

"**No other source provides the same level of coverage.** Because users would want and need to read through the entire source, it is recommended that (this volume) be **included in the circulating collection as well as the reference departments of school, public, and academic libraries.**"
— *RQ*

"**More than a standard reference tool** for those seeking to enter the field of advertising, this is a readable book made up of short articles by advertising executives at both large and small firms. Unlike many career guides, it provides an **insider's view** of the profession ... **Highly Recommended**"
— *Library Journal*

"The authors uniformly offer an insider's view...This sort of information presented by **credible** authorities is **more useful** to students choosing careers than are the very general descriptions of occupations in the Dept. of Labor's *Occupational Outlook Handbook* and its legion of imitators."
— *Wilson Library Bulletin*

"Its **on target**. A gem for professionals who are asked, 'Can I talk to you about getting a job in public relations?' Or who are thinking about making a move themselves. **A must** for school libraries and students eager for info on jobs in the profession."
— *pr reporter*

"...**excellent essays** on various occupations, each written by an expert in the field."
— *Career Opportunities News*

"For anyone wanting to break into magazine publishing or desiring to increase his or her current status in the field, this may be **the definitive volume.**"
— *Booklist*

"Another **excellent** volume in your **outstanding** series."
— Carolyn Lindquist, Coordinator of Library Resources, Cornell Univ. Career Center

"The articles are by folks who **know their fields inside and out. An exhaustive** volume that tells you just about **anything you want to know about the field.**"
— *The Book Reader*

"Students and alumni have found your (Career Directories) **packed full of insight and information**...an **essential** part of our resource center."
— Gerrie Campbell, Career Information Services, Univ. of Iowa

"...this data is difficult and time-consuming to obtain elsewhere. (These books) provide **more specific information** than is usually found...Useful for **career resource collections, or for counselors, journalism departments, career advisors or young people.**"
— *Choice*

"Very clear, concise explanation of internships available in the areas listed in each volume. Offers **more information on internships in these specialized areas than any book ever published.**"
—*ARBA 89*

"Geographical coverage is wide (**locations outside New York City are well represented).**"
—*Library Journal*

The Career Directory Series

Advertising Career Directory, Fourth Edition. (224 pp.,ISBN 0-934829-59-4, $19.95)

Book Publishing Career Directory, Fourth Edition. (224 pp., ISBN 0-934829-60-8, $19.95)

Business & Finance Career Directory, First Edition (256 pp., ISBN 0-934829-49-7, $19.95)

Healthcare Career Directory, First Edition (208 pp., ISBN 0-934829-83-7, $19.95)

Magazines Career Directory, Fourth Edition. (224 pp., ISBN 0-934829-61-6, $19.95)

Marketing & Sales Career Directory, Third Edition. (256 pp., ISBN 0-934829-62-4, $19.95)

Newspapers Career Directory, Third Edition. (224 pp., ISBN 0-934829-63-2, $19.95)

Public Relations Career Directory, Fourth Edition. (224 pp., ISBN 0-934829-64-0, $19.95)

Radio & Television Career Directory, First Edition (208 pp., ISBN 0-934829-82-9, $19.95)

Travel & Hospitality Career Directory, First Edition (256 pp., ISBN 0-934829-48-9, $19.95)

The Internships Series

Internships, Vol. 1: Advertising, Marketing, Public Relations & Sales,
Second Edition. (192 pp., 6 x 9, ISBN 0-934829-65-9, $11.95)

Internships, Vol. 2: Newspaper, Magazine & Book Publishing,
Second Edition. (224 pp., 6 x 9, ISBN 0-934829-66-7, $11.95)

Internships, Vol. 3: Accounting, Banking, Brokerage, Finance & Insurance,
First Edition (224 pp., 6 x 9, ISBN 0-934829-53-5, $11.95)

Internships, Vol. 4: The Travel & Hospitality Industries,
First Edition (224 pp., 6 x 9, ISBN 0-934829-52-7, $11.95)

Internships, Vol. 5: Radio & Television, Broadcasting & Production,
First Edition (224 pp. [est.], 6 x 9, ISBN 0-934829-84-5, $11.95)

Available at your local library, your favorite bookstore, or directly from the publisher, The Career Press

1st Edition

RADIO & TELEVISION
Career Directory

The Career Directory Series

Edited by Ronald W. Fry

The Career Press
180 Fifth Avenue
PO Box 34
Hawthorne, NJ 07507
1-800-CAREER-1
FAX: 201-427-2037

The Career Directory Series

Radio & Television Career Directory, First Edition

Paperback ISBN 0-934829-82-9, $19.95

Copies of this Directory may be ordered by mail or phone directly from the publisher. To order by mail, please include price as noted above, $2.50 handling per order, plus $1.00 for each book ordered. (New Jersey residents please add 7% sales tax.) Send to:

The Career Press Inc.
180 Fifth Avenue., PO Box 34,
Hawthorne, NJ 07507

Or call Toll-Free 1-800-CAREER-1 to order using your VISA or Mastercard or for further information on all books published or distributed by The Career Press.

Table of Contents

RADIO & TELEVISION
Career Directory

Section One: Advice From The Pros

Section Two: The Job Search Process

Section Three: Job Opportunities Databanks

Section Four: Appendices & Index

Section 1

Advice From The Pros

1

Becoming A Radio Personality—
My Career And Yours

Interview with Rodger Skibenes, Newscaster/Reporter
WOR Radio, New York

The following interview with Rodger Skibenes—newscaster/reporter for WOR Radio in New York—is especially pertinent to those of you interested in being "on the air," in any capacity, at a radio or TV station.

Q. What first interested you in radio?

A. I was just fascinated by it. I always wanted to get into radio, ever since I was in grade school. On the hour lunch breaks that we had, I would hurry and eat my food, then run down to the local radio station and just sit and watch the staff announcer. It was a very small studio and control room. If you worked there, you did everything yourself—ran your own records, read your own news, read your own spots, you were it! And that's the way most of the small town radio stations are today. But I was absolutely fascinated by the whole process.

Q. Tell me about how you started your career.

A. Let's face it, life was a little dull in Northern Minnesota, just below the Canadian border. I knew at a very young age that I wanted to be involved with radio. I started in 1956 as a staff announcer in Minneapolis. I was a senior in high school and got my first experience by accident. Our school had a program on a radio station and I was chosen as the announcer. I got my break there, then worked at many radio stations and some television stations. I started as a staff announcer, then evolved into what we now call a disc jockey, then went into news. I have worked in Chicago, Boston and New York.

I made the switch to news in 1961. I had been doing both news and music at a formatted station. I decided to go into news when I looked around and realized there were a million disc jockeys. Back in those days all radio stations had news, and I was attracted to it.

Radio news has evolved tremendously—it goes all the way from little stations that just rip it off the machine and read it, to larger stations that have large staffs working on the information. WOR has a comparatively large staff.

But it's nothing compared to what it was fifteen years ago. There were maybe thirteen writers at the station. Back in those days you get could a job at the big radio stations and make lots of money by simply being able to read the news. Somebody else would write it. You would come in twenty-five minutes before air, read it over, sit down and go.

Now most writers are gone, because you do not have just *readers*. Even at the networks—I worked at ABC network radio—you write your own newscasts. If you can't write, you can't be on the air. It's as simple as that.

The incredibly advanced technology (computers, etc.) have a lot to do with all the changes. In the old days (way back), they actually took in reports from correspondents and put them on a disc, like a record. Then, of course, it changed to tape (reel-to-reel), which was also very cumbersome. Now, using the cassette and simplified taping procedures, reporters will give you a report and you simply put it on the air. It's all very fast.

Q. **What is a typical day like for you?**

A. I leave for work at 2:30 in the morning, and I'm in the studio by 3:15 A.M. (My hours have always been crazy, and you don't get off on most holidays.) With my cup of coffee, I have a conference with the overnight editor to find out what's been happening and what's the latest. I check to see what was left by the local reporters for morning use. I find out what's been sent to all the ABC affiliates over a closed circuit from all over the world. Then I go through the papers and see what news to report, depending on what's "hot" that day. After that, I go through the wire copy that's been received in the newsroom by the various wire services.

I then write up the stories that I've decided to use. I generally write the 6:00, 7:00, 8:00, 9:00 and 10:00 AM newscasts. There are always new developments to report in a city like New York. Of course, if there is a lot of news, you have to decide which items to omit. There are certain things the public *must* know, other things they might *want* to know.

Q. **What are some ways a person can get started in a radio career?**

A. First of all, find an internship. Work as an intern for a station, and if you're good, the station cannot do without you. You take so many responsibilities and details off of other employees, they know that if you go and someone else comes in, it will be awful. A new person needs to be trained again. The benefit for interns is that they get to work next to people that know what they're doing, and they can learn a lot while they are there. They can often go out with a reporter to see what happens and why and learn some things that way. Most interns are in college and find positions through the career office at school. The intern is a very important person.

Another way to get started is to research certain trade publications—such as *Radio & Records, Broadcasting Magazine*, and a pamphlet from the American Federation of Television and Radio Artists (AFTRA), which have job listings. Whatever information you can get is useful, even though some listings are only for experienced people. A small market will take someone with little experience and let them start out there. In fact, I recommend starting out in a small market where you have to do everything. If you're willing to work, even when the pay is horrible, you'll get the experience you need to move on. This is where to make mistakes and learn from them. Prepare to sacrifice some things—maybe moving away from family. If you're really motivated, it won't go unnoticed...you're preparing to work up the ladder.

Q. What education should a person have when considering such a career?

A. For radio or television news—you're education is really "life." Is a college degree important? Yes. Is it absolutely necessary? No. If you go to college, you want to get as much in the areas of history (American and European), literature, and English as possible. Journalism is good, too, and there are some excellent schools. You want to know as much as you can *about* as much as you can. Invariably, as you go about reporting and covering the news, things are going to come up that you'll only know through your personal experience or because you read it some place. In this business, almost everything you have done, seen or experienced is brought up by covering day-to-day news.

   Successful programming hosts like John Gambling, Howard Stern or Don "Imus in the Morning" are bright people, and they are very well read, up-to-date on almost everything. To be successful in this field, you can't just close your eyes and be happy watching television—you have to read continuously and learn as much as possible.

Q. What if you have all the education and appropriate skills to be on radio, but you don't have that "winning" voice?

A. In all honesty, "voice" is becoming less and less important these days. You can have a pleasant voice, but you do not have to have a *super* voice. Don't let that be a handicap in your pursuit of a career. If you are qualified in all other areas, your voice can be worked on. Stations prefer to hire people for news without accents, except for maybe the disc jockeys. That's not to say that you can't have a flavor of an accent, but it can't be overwhelming.

Q. Describe an ideal candidate.

A. Curious and wants to learn, one who is interested in current events, and has the motivation. The person should be a good student and a reader—noticing the world around them. I can't stress that enough.

Q. Are there any specific areas of training?

A. For electronic journalism, whether radio or television, there are programs available at colleges. You must have good writing skills. Generally you develop this ability in school, or getting the break as an intern in a newsroom when someone can show you how to write. I know someone who was hired as a desk assistant at WABC working with me and another fellow, and he learned how to write by observing and reading what we wrote. He would then submit copy and we would critique his work. But he learned, and now he's working at one of the network TV stations.

Q. What should someone starting a career in radio expect in the way of salary their first year?

A. Not much, but be patient. If you develop your skills, you're providing for your future. You want to make sure that when you move up, you are indeed qualified for that job. otherwise it can set you back. Make sure you have a grasp of what you are and what you can do before you move on. But be confident. Depending on the size of the market, you can make money as you go up. Big stations will have big salaries once you move up. The field is wide open, and for good talent, stations will pay.

Q. Is there a ladder to climb?

A. Definitely, you've got to begin by gaining the experience, that is the first rung. Let's use a small market as an example: Sioux Falls, South Dakota. You could get a job developing your skills, whether it's in news, on the air as a disc jockey, or perhaps by convincing the program director to do a talk show. All of this is experience, and if you get better as a result of this, you may go from that station to Fargo, North Dakota (which is bigger) and you'll make more. As you gain more experience and you do an incredible job there, who knows, you might get snatched up by Minneapolis. With the experience you've gotten and the skills you've defined, you're on your way to the bigger places with more opportunities.

Q. If someone were to leave a career in radio, what other jobs might they be prepared for?

A. If you were in radio or television journalism, you can become very good at PR work. State agencies, federal agencies and elected officials love to use people who have previously been in the news arena, since they know something about what they're saying—they know what the issues are and where to find them. Also, if you were on talk radio and you have a good personality, you might do well in certain sales areas. You have the ability to communicate and that is very important.

Q. Would you recommend a radio career to someone who is genuinely interested? And if so, why?

A. I would say make sure you definitely want to do it, because jobs in radio news reporting are slimming down. Since deregulation, a lot of stations aren't even bothering with news. Some read five minutes of news and that's it. Back in the old days, the news department was staffed 24 hours a day, so you can imagine how the job market has shrunk. In some instances, you can get into the "all news" stations, like WINS and WCBS in New York. But for that you have to have a lot going for you. Everything falls back on the basic skills and determination you have. And again, I can't stress enough the fact that you should be well read.

I sometimes say that radio broadcasting or journalism is not really a profession—there are no set legal standards that say: "In order to be a journalist in New York, you must have an MA degree and have "X" number of hours on the job." Being a journalist is like being a carpenter—it's a trade. You have developed your skills and put them to work. Generally, the more you work at it, the more dedicated and talented you become.

RODGER SKIBENES is currently the morning news anchor on "Rambling With Gambling" on WOR Radio in New York.

2

Careers In Radio And Television News

Radio-Television News Directors Association

Electronic journalists work in a field as vital as the world around us. From reporters, photographers and producers to managers and anchorpersons, their job is to transmit "actuality"—the sights and sounds of events as they happen, of history as it's made. Television gives the viewer a seat at a Senate hearing, a safe view of armed conflict in a distant nation, details of what's happening around the corner. Radio lets us follow the progress of a tornado, tells us when to expect the power to come back on, or exposes us to diverse opinions. Radio and television journalists are in the middle of it all.

Technology has expanded our potential for reporting and will continue to do so. Live satellite coverage of disasters, ceremonies or sports can now originate from another part of the state or another continent...without anyone seeing much difference. Reporters and news sources scattered all over the world can talk with one another as if they were in the same studio.

But despite all the gizmos and gadgets, the main component of news will remain bright, innovative women and men whose job it is to report and make sense of events and conditions in local communities, the nation and the world.

An Always Exciting Career

For many, working with news never gets old. Dan Rather of CBS News, a broadcast journalist for more than 30 years, says, "I love it. I'm excited about it every day. This is not cheerleading. This is real appreciation that I have such a good job."

Newcomers with the required education and ability can usually find jobs in radio or TV news if they are willing to start at the bottom of the totem pole with salaries that are undeniably spartan. Sorry, but forget the million dollar-plus salaries commanded by a few star anchors. Dan Rather started, like most, at the bottom—earning minimum wage (then 75 cents an hour) at a small radio station in Texas in the early 1950s. (But keep reading—the money improves quickly if you've got what it takes!)

Jobs are always opening up. An estimated 38,000 people were working in news at commercial radio and TV stations in the late 1980s—9,000 of them had been hired within the previous 12 months. Several hundred of these were beginners on their first full-time jobs in broadcast news.

But it's a competitive field, and aspirants may fail to get or keep jobs if they and the jobs are not right for each other. So assess your natural inclinations and your potential. If you decide on electronic journalism, give it your best and see how well you do. If it doesn't turn out, there are many other careers your journalistic talents will help you pursue. And your time will not have been wasted. The communication skills you learn in radio or TV news will make you more effective in most jobs in other fields.

Where The Jobs Are

Surveys indicate that people want more news and public affairs coverage by radio and television and will be turning to electronic media increasingly in the years ahead. And there are a lot of places for them to turn:

Commercial TV stations are a primary source of news. About 750 of these stations have local news operations. Nationwide, the average network affiliate TV station employs about 23 people to work in news. About half of the independent TV stations (those not affiliated with ABC, CBS or NBC) have news staffs, typically four or five people.

Commercial radio stations in the United States number about 9,000. Most of them originate local news, though the number of news operations is only about 6,000 because the same news staff often serves two stations—jointly owned AM and FM. The average radio news staff consists of one full-time person and one part-timer.

Public television offers alternatives to regular commercial fare. The Public Broadcasting Service (PBS) produces an hour-long evening TV newscast ("The MacNeil/Lehrer NewsHour"). Few of the nation's approximately 300 non-commercial TV stations have local newscasts, but many do local public affairs programming.

Public radio stations number about 1,250, of which more than 500 broadcast to a general audience and have news operations. The majority of these stations are served by the National Public Radio or American Public Radio network. At both the network and station level, public radio tends to report significant stories in greater depth than commercial radio.

Broadcast networks employ several thousand newspeople, but they seldom hire anyone lacking experience at a local station.

Cable television (CATV) is opening new jobs in broadcast journalism through cable news and information networks and expanded TV service to local communities. 8,000 cable systems now serve more than 60 percent of the nation's TV households, though most do not have news staffs. But that's changing. CATV systems in a growing number of cities put on their own local news operations. For example, 300,000 New York-area subscribers are served by Cablevision Systems' "Long Island News 12," a 24-hour news operation employing more than 40 people. A number of other CATV systems, even small ones, have gotten into local news programming (albeit on a smaller scale). Cable information networks such as Cable News Network (CNN) and Financial News Network (FNN) also employ journalists.

Corporate television is a growing field, as large businesses increasingly send programs they produce to their workers—within the same buildings or, by satellite, to plants and offices anywhere in the world. At least one pizza chain beams policies and helpful hints throughout its system via communication satellite.

The wire services, which provide news to broadcast stations and newspapers 24 hours a day, employ hundreds of journalists. For their broadcast wires and networks, Associated Press and

United Press International generally prefer to hire TV and radio newspeople rather than retrain newspaper reporters or editors.

Public relations—A field that helps industries, organizations and government communicate with the public finds employees who are trained and experienced in broadcast news to be most attractive.

Technology is changing the tools in electronic journalism and related fields. In computerized newsrooms, video display terminals have replaced typewriters. And instead of tearing paper off news wire machines, you just punch up stories on a screen. Computers also generate graphics and make the editing of news tape easier and more precise. Outside the newsroom, cameras are becoming more compact, simpler to operate and more durable.

But technology will not replace the reporters, writers, editors, producers and supervisors who are at the heart of news operations. Computers and satellites are only tools to help people do their jobs.

What The Jobs Are

Jobs, positions and titles vary from station to station, but some of the people typically found in broadcast news operations include:

Reporter. An originator of news stories; the person who gets the interviews and other information that *are* the news. Reporters must be effective at interviewing government officials and other people who make news. They need to be well versed in the stories they cover, which involves the expert use of information from periodicals, wire services and, increasingly, computerized data bases. Broadcast reporters bring together these elements into a concise and cohesive format that uses words, sound and pictures to communicate the event or condition. Anchorpersons normally come from the ranks of reporters.

Cameraperson (photojournalist, photographer). Operator of ENG (electronic news gathering) camera used in visual reporting of news. May also have other reportorial duties, especially in smaller operations. Edits or helps edit tape at many stations.

Assignment editor. The coordinator who keeps track of scheduled and unscheduled news events and assigns reporters and photographers to cover them. Monitors police radio broadcasts, takes phone calls from news sources, must make quick decisions, often under severe time pressure. Maintains field contact with reporters and photojournalists through two-way radio and phone. Usually central in scheduling and overseeing satellite feeds of news stories. This job is one of the toughest and may be a steppingstone to higher management in a newsroom.

News producer. Behind-the-scenes journalist who combines live and taped actualities of events plus graphics and background information into a news story and coordinates stories into news programs. Writes news stories and lead-ins to them. May edit tapes and prepare graphics. News producers are creators, decision-makers and often managers who must be expert in many aspects of TV news. The job really can get as hectic as it did for the fictional producer played by Holly Hunter in the movie "Broadcast News."

Executive news producer. Overall supervision of news producers and coordinator of production elements of news programs. Often chief producer of principal news program. Works with news director on matters of program format and content, production financial budget and personnel performance. Executive news producers often move up to become new directors.

Writer. Journalist who writes news copy from information gathered from news teletype services, network feeds, interviews, recordings, documents and other information sources. In many operations, most writing is done by producers, reporters and anchors, not by separate writers.

Tape editor. One who selects and assembles those portions of audio or video tape which best tell a news story. Tape editing is also done by photographers, producers and reporters.

Anchorperson (newscaster). The on-air reporter who presides over a news program—reporting stories, introducing reports by others, and often interacting with other news, sports or weather anchors. Must get segments on and off on time. In some cases, may be managing editor or producer of the program.

New director. The person in charge of a TV or radio news operation. This journalist and manager sets policies and makes decisions regarding news coverage and presentation, recruits and trains personnel, develops and manages a departmental budget, and coordinates the relationship of the news department with other parts of the station. News directors in radio and small-market television often also do reporting, producing or anchoring.

Assistant news director. Second in command, this person helps the news director with managerial or journalistic work and is in charge when the news director is away. In some operations, this job may be handled by an executive producer or assignment editor.

Other job titles include *chief photographer, assignment desk assistants, assistant* and *associate producers, special projects producer* and *managing news editor.* (The latter position is found in a limited number of operations and may range from a program's chief editor/producer to a news director's second-in-command for news matters.)

Sports and weather are part of the news operation at some stations, separate at others, though audiences who see them sharing a news anchor desk still tend to think of them as part of the news team.

Your First (And, Hopefully!) Later Jobs

In TV news, the most common entry-level assignment for broadcast and electronic news graduates is *field reporting*—getting out where the news *is.* Less often, the first job may be as a producer or production assistant (generally at smaller stations). Most stations prefer that their producers first get some background in reporting. After all, reporting is the foundation upon which everything else in a news operation is constructed.

Photojournalism also provides entry-level jobs. Some news camerapersons are true photojournalists, professionals who use cameras to show the realities that are news and who position themselves for advancement in the field. Others, perhaps without college degrees, are primarily technicians who shoot exactly what reporters and producers tell them to shoot. Reporters at small stations are often expected to use cameras as part of their reporting chores.

In radio, first jobs in small and medium markets typically combine reporting and newscasting. Working with tape recordings of news events and interviews is required. The radio newscaster normally edits actualities (the sound of newsmakers), writes, edits and produces his or her program. Few of the large news operations in major markets such as New York or Chicago hire staff just out of college. When they do, the assignments normally are writing, desk or production assistance, or other inside jobs.

Bigger Isn't Necessarily Better

A danger of starting in a major market is that jobs there tend to be so specialized that it's easy to get stuck in a low-level inside job when you would prefer to be out reporting. It may be hard to get reassigned. Large operations usually hire their reporters from among those who have gained reporting experience at smaller stations.

Versatility, an asset for anyone, is best developed in a small or medium operation, where you can report, write, go on the air, take part in the production of stories, even learn to use a camera. The smaller the news staff, the more likely that you would do several kinds of jobs each week. This permits you try a variety of news positions to see which you're most suited for (and prefer).

Most reporters at the station level are on general assignment, but there are opportunities for specialists in such areas as business, consumer and health reporting. Specialization is most pronounced at large stations and the networks, but many small TV and radio stations also do specialized reporting.

The small-market radio news director is a generalist, often a one-person band who keeps up with the community, gathers news, writes it, edits tape and goes on the air with it.

You Won't Be Dan Rather Tomorrow

Be advised that very few beginners start out as TV anchorpersons. The normal progression is for a reporter who comes across well on the air to break into anchoring on weekend or daytime weekday newscasts. Only after successfully developing yourself at that level will you have much chance of getting one of the regular early or late evening anchor assignments to which you may aspire. If you want to go on the air as a newscaster right away, your best bet is to break into radio news in a small or medium market.

What about starting in radio and moving to television after a year or two? Radio can give solid experience in writing, on-air delivery, interviewing, first-hand reporting and the live, on-your-feet reporting of spot news which is becoming more and more important in both radio and television. Radio thus provides a training ground for fundamentals in either medium. But many TV news directors are so visually oriented that they prefer people who have worked in television from the start. Though opinions on this differ, if your real goal is TV news, your safest bet may be to try for an entry-level reporting job at a TV station in a small market.

The Pay—It Gets Better!

Salaries in broadcast news vary widely, depending on whether the station is radio or television, how many people work in the news operation, the size of the market, and what, in particular, you have to offer. Able, imaginative, dependable radio and TV journalists who give their jobs that "little extra" that spells quality are always in demand...often at attractive salaries.

Entry-level salaries in radio and TV news are generally comparable to those paid by daily newspapers—typically about $13,000 to $14,000. Higher starting pay may go to graduates who held part-time or summer jobs in radio or TV news while in school, because they should require less "breaking in."

Modest pay is to be expected at least for a year or two as you gain experience and develop your talents. No matter how well you do in school, you'll become a really valuable professional only by working in a full-time job. Normally, if you develop well for a year or so, you should be ready for a substantial salary increase at your station or another one.

Stars don't make all the money. News directors have higher salaries than rank and file anchorpersons at most stations and make about the same as average anchors in the 25 largest markets (from No. 1, New York, to No. 25, San Diego). In those major markets, however, *star* anchors, the highest paid at their stations, earn much more that their bosses. The highest-paid anchors in those same top 25 markets in 1988 averaged $182,000, compared to $88,400 for news directors.

Producers generally average a little more than reporters, but the ceiling is higher for reporters. Network-affiliated TV stations in the 25 largest markets typically paid their top reporter $54,100 and their top producer $41,500.

Salaries are normally two to three times as much in major TV markets as in small ones. Anchors make five times as much in major markets. The cost of living is also higher in larger markets, though normally not more than twice as much.

You'll probably do best in dollars, as well as career satisfaction, by doing what you do best. A good producer who moves up to a major operation or becomes a news director will earn more than a hack anchor who can never expect to make the big time.

If you're looking primarily for the fastest track to the Big Bucks, then sales or management training is probably a better career move than news.

Is It For You?

To get ahead in radio or TV news, you need to be an educated, literate, inquisitive, clear-thinking, cool-headed person who can get along with people, interview news sources, gather news, write well and tell stories effectively to the listener or viewer. You must develop a sense of what news is and be able to put it in perspective, which requires a solid understanding of current and historical events.

Personal presentation skills should also be developed. In broadcasting, unless you wish to work strictly behind the scenes, your voice and appearance should be acceptable for effective interviews and on-the-spot reports. Golden voices and glamorous faces are *not* required, but you must come across authoritatively and pleasingly. Most news departments want reporters who can cover the news and tell about it in a straightforward, easily understood manner.

If your goal is to become a "news announcer" or "news reader," you may be disappointed. There is little market for people who can only "parrot" the news. Most of the anchorpersons you see on local stations and the major networks are *not* news *readers*. They are journalists—reporters, writer and editors—who also go on the air. They write much of their own copy, report stories from the scene, and serve as newscast editors. The reason they look and sound as if they know what they are talking about is because they *do*.

How And When To Start

While in high school or college, start developing those abilities which are vital to the electronic journalist (though you'll find they'll help you in *any* career). Learn grammar, composition and clear expression—now. Don't wait until your first job, or even until college. At those levels, your supervisors or teachers will have better things to do than try to teach you high school English. So, first and foremost, learn the language.

Experience in public speaking or debate will help prepare you for on-air reporting. Learn typing and word processing. Read and observe as much as you can about all kinds of people and activities. Don't stop with assigned readings. Read books, magazines and newspapers. Become a critical listener and viewer of broadcast news. Experience with a school paper can be valuable. And perhaps there's part-time or freelance work in news, announcing or production at a local radio or TV station, on or off campus. Check the possibilities.

Visit stations in your area and observe their news operations (*do* call in advance to schedule a convenient time). Tag along with a reporter if possible. See how tape is edited and newscasts are put together. Observe the teamwork. See what it's all like and ask yourself if *you* would like to do it. Find out what opportunities there are for beginners to get experience at the stations. Get recommendations from professionals on where to go for an education.

Education

Whatever your college major, your emphasis during college should be on getting the broadest liberal arts education possible. About three-fourths of your courses should be in general studies or arts and sciences—history, political science, sociology, psychology, economics, literature, fine arts, etc. (The Accrediting Council on Education in Journalism and Mass Communication prescribes a ratio of roughly three such courses to every one in electronic journalism or other mass media areas.)

Avoid the trade school approach—taking course after course in "how to do" TV or radio, but few general education courses. Skill courses offered in a major can help give you a solid foundation for a career, but no number of classes can make you an experienced professional. Only full-time paid job experience can do that. It's easier to teach skills to an educated person on the job than to educate a skilled practitioner who missed out on liberal arts in school.

Consider broadcast and electronic journalism as a major which can combine a solid liberal arts education with basic skills training in a four-year undergraduate program. Our surveys have shown that TV and radio news directors prefer broadcast news majors to journalism or speech majors. But it's the program—not the name of the school or department—that counts. Some electronic journalism programs are found in units with names like telecommunications or mass communication.

Education in electronic journalism goes beyond skill courses. For example, your major may include a course in the law of mass communication. CBS's Dan Rather is among those who think it should. "For journalists and those who aspire to lifetimes practicing the profession, now more than ever a new emphasis on teaching the basics of the Constitution and the Bill of Rights is imperative," says Rather. "Journalists cannot defend the First Amendment if they do not know what it says."

Look for a school where students do advanced lab work in actual broadcast or cable news settings, rather than being limited to workbooks and "make-believe" labs.

You can get a head start in the job market by hands-on experience at a campus or commercial station while you're in school. Summer internships, other summer jobs or weekend work at off-campus radio or television stations will also set you on the right path to becoming a professional. Many stations use part-time help, jobs that sometimes lead to full-time positions.

Getting A Job

Start looking actively by early in your final term. You may have developed job leads or made contacts before then. But there's usually no point in formally applying for a job until you're within weeks of being ready to go to work. Most openings need filling promptly.

Cover all bases in looking for openings. Use your school's placement service. Watch job openings bulletin boards. Check ads in *Broadcasting* magazine and area publications. If you are a student member of the Radio-Television News Directors Association, you'll get listings from the our Job Information Service. Keep in touch with professors—they may hear of jobs, too.

Be realistic. Direct your efforts to stations that are likely to hire someone just out of school. Large operations seldom do. Some locations will be more attractive than others to you, but your first job may have to be in one that's less than ideal.

How selective should you be in applying? Advice varies. You may be counseled to take the shotgun approach and apply everywhere, just in case. But many of us advise limiting yourself to stations that are realistic prospects. Make a concentrated effort with those stations. If there's a station you are especially interested in, visit it. Even if there is no opening at the time, ask to see the operation. Personal contacts can pay off later.

Your job application letter should be businesslike, to the point, and addressed to the individual station or its news director by name, *not* a form letter. Try to keep it to a single page. Tell why you want the job, why you think you can do it, and when you will be available. If you're applying for a television job that may involve on-air reporting, note that a video cassette tape of your work is available. If it's radio, enclose an audio cassette tape. If the tape is unsolicited and you would like to have it returned, enclose a stamped return envelope.

Accumulate tapes of your work as evidence of how you come across on the air and put together a "resume tape." Reports from the scene tell the most about your potential as a field reporter. Include a sample of your newscasting for radio. That's okay for television, too, since it can indicate potential. But for a first job, the TV news director will probably look primarily at how well you report from a news scene.

Even if you do not have tapes of stories used on the air, you can still work up examples of how you perform as a reporter and newscaster. Just inform your prospective employer that they are "lab examples." News directors have limited time for auditioning tapes, so keep yours short—no more than 10-15 minutes. Put your best work, ideally field reporting for most applicants, up front—a strong lead can help keep you from getting cut off about one minute in. Make multiple copies of your audio or video resume tape. A few stations may want to keep yours on file for future consideration.

Examples of application letters, resumes and resume tapes may be available through the school's placement office. If you're turned down, keep trying.

If you really want to report the news, you won't let a couple of rejections keep you from keeping on!

The **RADIO-TELEVISION NEWS DIRECTORS ASSOCIATION** is the primary professional organization of broadcast and cable journalists. Members join to learn to do their jobs better and advance, to improve the quality of electronic journalism, and to protect press freedom. RTNDA acts as a "watchdog" to secure and protect the right to report the news to the public. The association sets standards for membership and makes annual awards for outstanding electronic journalism.

RTNDA publications help keep members on the cutting edge of the profession. The *Communicator*, a monthly magazine, carries articles of lasting value for electronic journalists, educators and students. *Intercom*, a bi-weekly newsletter, provides late news in the field. Members get listings from the RTNDA Job Information Service every two weeks in *Intercom*.

Student members of RTNDA at a number of universities have formed affiliates that hold meetings and engage in other professional activities. The Radio and Television News Directors Foundation finances scholarships for undergraduate and graduate students of electronic journalism, as well as fellowships for working electronic journalists new to the field who wish to enhance their professional background with academic studies.

3

The Show That Never Ends

Robert J. Dunphy, Vice-President—Programming
Mix 105-WNSR, New York City

Imagine yourself as the director of a 24-hours-a-day, seven-days-a-week, 365-days-a-year, non-stop movie...the plot of which changes daily.

And that the bulk of the material for your movie is being created by people you did not hire and cannot control (recording artists and record companies) in a time frame that you have no say about.

Finally, mix in a marketplace that generally consists of anywhere from five and eighty five competitors vying for a piece of your audience.

This will give you a sense of what it is like to be a radio station program director. And why radio programming is not for the faint of heart.

Build An Audience And...

The ultimate goal of the program director varies slightly depending on the size of the market, amount of competition, programming format and philosophy of the station owner.

In smaller markets, the job is relatively straightforward: to build a format and to create programming within that format that can be sold to advertisers. Generally speaking, the programming will consist of music combined with news, sports, weather, traffic and feature programs.

In many cases, the actual size of the ratings, or audience, is not as important as the quality of features and other programming. This is because you are creating radio "products" that can be put into sponsorship packages for advertisers.

The key to a successful small market station is having a wide variety of packages for the sales force to present directly to advertisers.

...Create Saleable Programs And Features

In the more competitive small markets and some medium markets, the job is two-fold: to build an audience for rating purposes *and* to create saleable programs and features. In these markets, ratings take on greater importance because of the competition. Ratings are a way for advertisers to choose one, two, three or more stations on which to place their commercials. (It is neither practical nor economically possible to buy advertising time on all of the stations in a market.) Also, advertising agencies become more of a factor in larger markets, and they prefer to deal with ratings as a way to justify their actions. However, saleable programs and features remain an important part of the programming.

In the largest markets, such as New York, the most successful stations focus their programming tactics almost exclusively on generating ratings. The reason for this is the heavy use of ratings by advertising agencies and the heavy use of advertising agencies by the businesses in those markets. Furthermore, the greater competition in these markets (there are over 70 radio stations in the New York area) requires a ratings system to "keep score" of the audience of all the stations.

Creating Your Own Training "Program"

Unlike many careers, there is very little formal training available to learn to become a radio programmer. The basic requirements for the job are an interest in music, people, popular culture, marketing and change. With these basics in mind, you can chart an educational course that will give you some of the skills you need to get started. While a degree in broadcasting probably will not hurt you, it might be better to minor in broadcasting and major in business or marketing.

This does not mean you should throw out the math and science courses. Radio ratings are statistics, and statistics by their very nature are math. Also, the technologies of broadcasting are physics and electronics, and it helps to know some fundamentals.

Finally, some background in education is very useful. You need to understand how people learn and become familiar with songs and products.

Typical Career Path

Radio is a wonderful business, but not everyone is a highly paid deejay or major market programmer. There are more than 10,000 commercial radio stations licensed in the United States, the vast majority of which are *outside* the major markets. There are many more people trying to break into radio than there are well-paying jobs. However, this does not mean you cannot break into the business—in fact, there is a shortage of skilled on- and off-air talent. But it does mean that in order to get your feet wet, you have to start in either a small market or a low-level job in a larger market.

In a small market, you probably will wear more than one hat. For example, if you are a deejay, you might also make commercials for advertisers or set up station promotions and contests. If you enjoy writing, you might be a copywriter for advertisers. In a smaller market, you will have the opportunity to work in and learn about a number of areas at the radio station—eventually, you will find all of this knowledge immensely useful. The down side to a small market is that the pay might not be as high as you would like. But then, virtually no one works in the programming side of radio just for the money.

In a larger market, the entry-level opportunities are different, because the higher level of competition creates the need for different skills. Here, you might start out as a request line operator, talking to listeners about their favorite songs and answering questions about contests. Or work in or supervise a "callout research" department responsible for calling listeners to survey their music and programming preferences. Or as an assistant in commercial production or promotion or programming.

It is important to get your foot in the door with someone who will teach you, or at least help you learn, about radio programming in general. If you get into a situation where you are not learning, you should consider moving on.

Once You're In The Door

Like any other business, you'll learn more on the job in radio than you ever could in school. Some of this comes from the formal training and indoctrination you receive upon being hired. However, in order to learn even more and advance more quickly, there are two key things you should do.

First, always give people a better, more thorough job than they expect. When you get an assignment, think about how you can give them not only what they expect or need, but something additional that can help them. They will appreciate the care and thought and extra effort you have given to their assignment, and you will have demonstrated that you understand more than they thought. Keep in mind that no one ever gets ahead by working "9 to 5."

Second, become a student of the business of radio. Study any and all trade magazines to which the station subscribes. Study not only programming, promotion and music, but sales, management, budget accounting and general business. The more you know, and the earlier you learn it, the higher you can go in your career.

Radio programming requires staying on top of popular culture and current events. It is not "WKRP In Cincinnati"—we do not run around in jeans and T-shirts listening to records. It requires a broad education and an interest in learning all the time. Radio programming also is an exciting job, filled with change.

ROBERT J. DUNPHY is vice president/programming of Mix105 WNSR, New York City, a Bonneville International Corporation station. He began his radio career at his college radio station at Northwestern University. He has supervised research at radio stations in Los Angeles and Philadelphia, programmed stations in central New Jersey, Cleveland and New York, and has consulted with radio stations and syndicated programs nationally.

4

Getting Started In Radio
~~Sales~~ Marketing

George C. Hyde, Executive Vice President
Radio Advertising Bureau

Without a Sales Department, there wouldn't be a radio station. It's just that simple.

There are more than 9,000 commercial radio stations in the United States, and their lifeblood is the revenue generated by the sale of commercials or programs to advertisers. Salaries for disc jockeys and talk-show hosts, capital acquisitions like studio equipment and transmitters, and operating expenses such as prizes for listener contests are all funded by the efforts of station salespeople—more than 65,000 strong.

Radio salespeople are an integral part of the American system of broadcasting, and their future has never been brighter. Radio sales is a highly mobile, fast-track occupation that can lead to management and ownership opportunities and six-figure incomes...but *after* you've "paid your dues," of course!

What's The Job?

At every level of a radio sales career, the job is essentially the same: Identify the marketing goals and needs of prospective advertisers, develop a radio marketing plan to meet those goals/needs, convince the prospect of the plan's value, and monitor implementation of the plan to insure success.

In an entry-level sales position, you're likely to spend a great deal of your time "cold calling" on the people who own and manage small- to medium-sized businesses in your station's coverage area. After you've overcome the first challenge (getting an appointment with the decision maker), you'll be expected to do some research on the general nature of the prospect's business before a face-to-face meeting.

When you get across the desk from the prospect for the first time, your emphasis should be on *asking questions* and *listening*, not on talking! The more you learn about a client's business needs and aspirations, the better you'll be at developing a successful radio marketing plan which addresses and satisfies those needs and aspirations!

After this "fact-finding mission" (or perhaps after *several* more), you'll have the client information you need to begin developing a radio marketing plan, selecting those features of your radio station which offer the appropriate benefits to the prospective advertiser. If you've asked the right questions and listened carefully, you will be successful in developing a plan which you will then present to the decision maker for approval.

Sounds Easy, Doesn't It?

Well, don't be so sure. There's more to do, because your responsibility doesn't stop when the sale is made. Particularly at an early stage of your career or in a smaller station or community, you'll also be responsible for writing the actual commercials and making sure they are broadcast on the days and times you've discussed with your client.

As one broadcasting sage once put it, "A sale isn't a sale until the check clears the bank," so there's another responsibility you'll encounter in a radio sales career—making sure the advertiser pays the bill in a timely fashion. Indeed, many stations do not pay commissions to their sales staffs until the clients have paid the stations…just in case you needed extra motivation!

Gradually, you will build up an "account list" of clients and prospects for whom you are the station's representative. While you can expect to remain involved with clients who are active advertisers, you should also understand that your sales manager has the ability—and the responsibility—to re-assign your inactive accounts to other salespeople, just as he or she may ask you to take over an account where another salesperson has not been successful.

Beyond Entry-Level

As your develop experience and expertise, you're likely to be assigned to deal with larger advertisers and with advertising agencies representing prospective clients. You'll be expected to have an understanding of quantitative audience measurement reports ("the ratings"), and, possibly, qualitative analyses of the composition of your station's audience, as well. In many cases, much of your in-person contact will be with the individuals assigned to negotiate price on the client's behalf, but the most successful radio salespeople are adept at maintaining relationships with the clients themselves, as well as with their agencies or media buyers.

The Career Track And Earning Potential

A career in radio sales definitely puts you on the "fast-track." Radio stations are constantly on the lookout for bright and aggressive salespeople to replace those who move along to greater responsibility. And the higher you go, the more you make…and the faster you make it. "How much?" you ask! First, you must realize that salespeople's compensation is based on the revenues they generate in advertising sales. In some cases, a salesperson receives a salary plus a commission on personal sales. But in many cases, the compensation is "straight commission"—a specific percentage of sales or collections, with little or no "guaranteed" income. If you're focused on the maximum upside earnings potential, you may find a straight commission scheme more to your liking. If you like guarantees, you'd probably be better off in another profession entirely (not just another sales job).

Here are some industry averages for salesperson compensation in various size markets, as reported by the National Association of Broadcasters and the Broadcast Financial Management Association:

Market Population	Annual Earnings/Salesperson
Under 25,000 persons	$17,825
50,000 to 99,999	$21,598
250,000 to 499,999	$28,852
500,000 to 999.999	$42,073
2,500,000 and above	$49,349

After a few successful years as a radio salesperson, you'll likely be confronted with (at least) one of these three opportunities:

A) Local sales manager's position at your station;

B) Sales position at a larger station in the same area; or

C) Sales position at a station in a larger market.

Certainly, there are a variety of personal and professional factors that will influence your choice. For the most part, the larger the market size, the larger the earning potential. Since that is likely to be a major factor in your decision, here's a look at compensation totals for local sales managers in a variety of market sizes:

Market Population	Annual Earnings/Local Sales Manager
Under 25,000 persons	$23,975
50,000 to 99,999	$34,145
250,000 to 499,999	$42,266
500,000 to 999.999	$56,784
2,500,000 and above	$86,230

Local sales managers are responsible for supervising the activities of the local sales staff and maximizing revenue from local clients. General sales managers typically oversee sales to national as well as local clients. General sales managers in the largest markets have average earnings in excess of $100,000.

About The Title Of This Article

Now that you've seen the "promised land," let's come back to entry-level, and deal with a couple of basics that will help you accelerate your radio career. Number One: It's time to stop talking about "radio *sales*." It's time to start talking about "radio *marketing*."

Selling radio time may solve the salesperson's problem, the sales manager's problem, and the station owner's problem. It doesn't necessarily do anything for the *client*. That's why it's an archaic concept. *Marketing* radio involves identifying and satisfying the clients' needs *through* sales. This is the arena for the professional radio marketing consultant of the present and future.

Hence, Number Two: Be ready to learn to be a marketing consultant. Forget the "Herb Tarlek" caricature of the radio salesperson on the old "WKRP in Cincinnati" sitcom. The future of radio marketing belongs to a new breed of professional marketing consultants, one that understands that the strongest and most rewarding long-term marketing relationships focus first on satisfying clients' needs.

In an earlier age, Herb and his back-patting cronies could build a career on a firm hand-shake, big smile, good jokes, and a generous expense account. Not so today. Too much is at stake for business decision makers to trust their advertising investments to people who are ill-informed about their business goals.

Education and Professional Development

While there are no strict educational requirements for a career in radio, you should concentrate on building your general knowledge of business and marketing. The more courses and seminars you take to broaden your understanding of how businesses operate and how they present their goods and services to the public, the better prepared you'll be to demonstrate to your prospects the benefits they'll enjoy when they make radio a key component of their advertising plans.

Many radio stations, broadcasting groups, and associated industries offer summer student internships, an opportunity to gain "hands-on" experience that can accelerate your career in radio marketing. Contact your state broadcasters association or the National Association of Broadcasters (Washington, DC) for further information on internships or write directly to stations and related organizations in your area. *(The most complete listing of internships at radio and television stations throughout the U.S. and Canada is now available in the brand-new **Internships, Volume 5: Radio & Television, Broadcasting & Production**, just published by The Career Press—Ed.)*

Professional development extends far beyond formal education, of course, and the Radio Advertising Bureau offers a wide variety of career-enhancement programs, beginning with the "Radio Sales University," a concentrated two-day curriculum for newcomers to radio marketing. RAB also presents a regular series of educational seminars in various cities across the country, as well as a Graduate Sales Management Program in conjunction with the Wharton School of Business at the University of Pennsylvania.

Many radio stations today are strongly encouraging their staffs to qualify for the CRMC (Certified Radio Marketing Consultant) designation, a program administered by the Radio Advertising Bureau. Similar in concept to the insurance industry's CLU (Certified Life Underwriter) designation, the CRMC identifies our industry's outstanding performers based on their knowledge and experience. Radio marketers may register for the CRMC exam after two years in the industry and must pass a comprehensive examination to qualify.

Radio Marketing In The Future

Radio marketing offers the opportunity to blend creativity with practical business thinking, combining attractive financial rewards with the satisfaction of helping businesses grow in our unique, entrepreneurial American economy.

The 1990s may well see a new "Golden Age" of Radio, at least from a marketing and sales standpoint. The intensity of business competition today requires the use of advertising media which target prime consumer prospects with rifle-shot accuracy, and not costly scattershot coverage.

Radio meets this requirement better than any other major medium. That's one reason why radio's share of total advertising in the United States continues to grow, and why the future is so bright for those of you who embark on a career in radio marketing right now.

GEORGE HYDE has been executive vice president of the Radio Advertising Bureau since September, 1989. He joined RAB after a 24-year career with Susquehanna Broadcasting. From 1982 to 1989, Mr. Hyde was regional vice president and general manager of WQBA-AM and FM, Miami, Florida, two of the most successful Spanish-language stations in the United States. Under his management, WQBA-AM and FM were recognized as inaugural winners of the NAB's "Crystal Award" for outstanding local service, and the "Marconi Award" for "Spanish Station of the Year" in 1989.

Mr. Hyde has been active in a variety of industry organizations, and served on the executive committee of the National Association of Broadcasters as vice chairman/radio in 1988-89, and on the NAB board from 1985 to 1989. A former president of the South Florida Radio Broadcasters Association, Mr. Hyde was also a member of the board and executive committee of the Florida Association of Broadcasters, and chaired the FAB Advertising Tax Committee that led the successful fight to repeal the Florida Services Tax. He continues to serve on the United Press International Broadcast Advisory Board.

Mr. Hyde has also been active in civic affairs, especially in the area of drug abuse awareness. He served as a national advisor to the White House Conference for a Drug-Free America, and as a director of Informed Families of Dade County, Florida. A graduate of Brown University, Mr. Hyde also holds a Master's degree in business administration.

5

Becoming A Producer Isn't Hard...
Unless You Want To Be A *Good* One

Kate Wood, Producer
Burkewood Communications Corp.

Excellent producers must have at least three talents—knowing how to communicate, how to manage and how to motivate.

They must be able to fully understand and become excited about the objectives of a project.

They must build a team of specialists (technicians, scriptwriters, camera crews, editors, etc), communicate the project prerequisites and inspire the team to give each project their all.

Producers, in other words, are the glue that binds everything and everyone together.

What Makes A *Good* Producer?

Good producers are good listeners. They understand each client's needs and meld those needs with the creative input of the production team.

Good producers are decisive and able to handle all of the problems that inevitably arise during the course of a project with good grace.

If, at the end of a project, the producer hears the client say to his or her boss, "I want you to see *my* program," the producer has accomplished his or her goal. Good producers get their satisfaction from the client's pride, not their own.

Being a producer means forgetting about "9-to-5" days and five-day weeks. Videotaping and editing can go on at any time within a 24-hour period. Sometimes you will need to be at the taping sessions and the editing sessions—whenever they're scheduled.

Sometimes, being a producer means doing the menial jobs—helping to build the set or bring in the food.

The only times producers are surprised is when things run well and on time, so make sure you are flexible enough to deal with change.

Assessing Your Skills And Talent

If you are considering a production career, my first advice would be to think back over your school years and (admittedly limited) job experience—identify what you did, and did *well*, and what you *like* to do. If you believe that you communicate, manage and motivate well—and can prove it through solid accomplishments in school or on the job—keep reading. You may have the makings of a good producer.

Looking back, I think I had the makings of a producer for most of my life. As a toddler, I organized my crib toys. All through high school and college, I took on leadership roles with the student government. In my professional life, I took positions in which I could lead a team—listening, managing and motivating. Until fifteen years ago, I was in school administration. Though my medium has changed—from the classroom to producing video programs for corporate and institutional clients—I don't feel that I've changed professions, because I'm still teaching, still motivating.

Liking what you are doing professionally is very important. If you are not enjoying yourself, you may not do a good job, and it will certainly be hard to motivate your team. Be sure you'll *like* being a manager and communicator.

And Taking The Proper Steps

The field is a very competitive one and, as in all careers and industries, luck and timing have something to do with when and how one gets ahead. There are, however, certain beneficial steps which you can take.

While In College, Study Liberal Arts

You must be able to listen to people's ideas and express your own, so take liberal arts courses—history, English, art, music—that will broaden your understanding of the many kinds of people who will be working with you in your career. Become involved in extracurricular activities where you can store up your managing and communicating skills. There are many opportunities on college campuses to become involved in video production. Don't start out trying to be a producer—start out as a crew member.

And don't shy away from so-called menial chores—they may be the best way to learn how a production team should function and what the various roles are within the team. You'll be a much better manager if you know the problems—and the good moments—each member of the team may encounter.

Become Familiar With The Specialties

Take a variety of technical production courses so you understand the production process. You do not need to be a wizard camera person or a sound/lighting engineer, but understanding their capacities will help you immensely in managing their tasks as a producer, and will give you the tools to get your foot in the door initially.

Apprenticeships

Seek out opportunities for on-the-job training. While most of these will be without pay, they will be invaluable opportunities to learn practical skills and to see whether you really like the career you're heading for.

Make A Good Impression

Leave college knowing that the college community (professors, administration, student body) believes in your dedication to your career. Your grades should be average to above average and you should have grabbed at opportunities to gain practical experience in TV production...and excelled in them. You are a team player and have gained some positive leadership experience.

Climbing The Career Ladder

I don't know anyone who *started out* as a producer. What you need to do is to get your foot in the door and show that you can make a positive contribution. Let your prospective employer know what your skills and ambitions are, but that what you really want is the opportunity to make a positive impact on his or her business and learn the job.

Some very good receptionists have become very good producers. Be patient with yourself, but always be persevering and on the lookout.

Keep an eye out for opportunities where you can make a difference. If you do this consistently—and do a good job when you are given the chances—more and more such opportunities will come your way. You may have to do some moonlighting in the beginning, but that will be a test of your own commitment to the profession.

You Can Do It

There is nothing easy about launching a production career or, for that matter, keeping it afloat. But if it's right for you, and you will find that out in time, you'll have some real satisfactions in your professional career.

Producers can work as employees of a company or as freelancers. It's likely that you will gain your credentials by working your way up through various jobs within a corporate production team. Keep a good record of the tasks you perform on each production and of the producers you work for (who, hopefully, will write credible recommendations for you as you build your resume). Once you have built your track record, freelancing can become an option.

The power of video is strong and becoming stronger. It is not hard work to *become* a producer. But it is very hard work to become a *good* producer.

Never give up on the opportunity to learn from others. And never miss a chance to let the right person know what you can do.

KATE WOOD is president of Burkewood Communications Corp., a video production company in Princeton, New Jersey. Burkewood is a family business. The other principal in the company is her husband John. Gil, their son, is a full-time Burkewood producer/director.

Kate began her television production career in 1978 when she founded the Educational Cable Consortium, a series on family issues for distribution on cable television. John and Kate founded Burkewood in 1985 to respond to the growing corporate and institutional need for video communications. As producers, Burkewood owns no equipment, so that clients can benefit from their communication and management skills while selecting the right team and equipment for each project.

A graduate of Wellesley College with a BA in history, Kate headed the Upper School at Kent Place School in Summit, New Jersey, before launching her television career.

6

Writing For Television: Infuriating Fun And Profitable Exhaustion

Claire Labine
Former Executive Producer & Headwriter—"Ryan's Hope"

Writing for television is something that thousands of people want to do...and with good reason: Television writers reach an audience of *millions*. In the best of circumstances, they have an unbelievable amount of fun. And make a lot of money.

Of course, in the *worst* of circumstances, the work is exhausting, infuriating and deleterious to their physical health and self esteem.

For now, let's ignore the "dark" side of this calling—you can deal with it if and when you actually make it as a writer. Let's worry instead about the *immediate* question: How do you establish yourself in a fiercely competitive market, one already full of talented, trained, and produced writers, a huge percentage of whom are chronically out of work?

Obviously, there's no formula for this, but if you have the desire, perseverance, and necessary degree of insanity to pursue a career in television writing, there are a number of ways you might begin.

The First Step

The best fundamental training is protracted study of dramatic writing at the college level. This typically will include courses in playwriting, screenwriting, and various television forms, all of which—sit-com, episodic, and long form, such as movies of the week and mini-series—have their own requirements.

The basis for all dramatic writing is an understanding of conflict, and, in my opinion, the best place to learn *that* is in a good playwriting course. If a full college program is not an option for you, at least start with a playwriting course. No one can teach you to write, but a good teacher can clarify some of the basic rules and, most importantly, make you *want* to write...and write...and write. And then write some more!

Practice Makes Perfect

Some people have a natural ear for dialogue, others don't. It's a skill that can be learned, and again, playwriting is the place to begin. Good dialogue is *not* the way *real* people *really* talk. It's a device that *sounds* like the way people talk, *vitalizes and illuminates* the characters, and *advances* the drama. The only way to learn to write dialogue is to *write* it. And then *listen* to it. If you have friends who are actors, do not hesitate to ask them to do readings of your work. In my experience, actors are the most generous people alive. They also learn by exercising their craft, and they respect writers. (After all, without us, they'd have no characters to play.) Their criticism can be enormously helpful.

The next step is to take your understanding of conflict and dialogue and move on to screenwriting, wherein you have a new tool, the camera, to enable you to tell your story, heighten the conflict, and define your characters.

Never Stop Watching...And Learning

While you're studying—and writing—go to the theatre. Go to the movies. See the same play or film two or three times, and bring your critical faculties with you. Why was *that* dramatic? Why (and how) were you moved? Why (and when) did you laugh?

Then apply all of the above to television. Tape your favorite series. Watch individual episodes until you understand the structure, the flow of the plot and sub-plot, and can hear the individual "voice" of each character. Write an outline. Write a script. Write another one.

Finding The Right Agent

The next step, ideally, is to find an agent. Not just any agent, but one who loves your work, likes you, and has time to promote you energetically. At this stage in your development—in the real world anyway—this rarely happens. In fact, I'm the only writer I know whose agent got me my first job in television...and all jobs since.

My playwriting professor at Columbia sent me a list of three agents, with an asterisk by the name of one. I called this individual and he agreed to read my work. I heard from him within a week (also unheard of in real life). Nothing I had sent him had any commercial value whatsoever, but he asked to see anything else I wrote. Needless to say, I obliged. None of *that* was saleable, either. He called every six weeks or so to inquire about my growing family, my husband, and what I was up to. This conduct, as far as I can tell, is unique in the history of show business.

Eventually, he learned of a staff opening on "Captain Kangaroo," vigorously promoted me for it, and arranged a writing audition. I got the job. He's been my agent for twenty-seven years and has become a cherished friend, dearly loved by all my family.

Showing The Right Work

I'm telling you this because it is every writer's fantasy, and it *did* happen to me. *But don't expect it to happen to you.* It is the exception, certainly *not* the rule.

You must, however, hope and try—and have good examples of your work to offer. A one-act play, in your own style, a reflection of your dramatic sensibilities, and a script designed for your favorite television series make a tidy package. Remember that a one-act play is faster to read than a screenplay. Anyone whose job involves stacks of reading appreciates short pieces. If you do submit a longer work to an agent, be sure the first ten pages are absolute dynamite.

Ask Other Writers

How do you get the name of an agent to whom to submit your work? If you don't know anyone who can recommend one, the Writer's Guild of America (East or West), will supply a list. Work your way through it. This will require time, postage, and multiple copies of your work (another good reason for short pieces).

Don't Be Afraid To Seek Help

This gets us to the subject of knowing people, which is how most writers get work. If your parents, siblings, friends, teachers, doctor, or dentist know a working writer, ask for an introduction and write a polite, but impassioned, letter imploring help. This can lead to further introductions to other writers, agents or producers. You should *not* be seeking (or even hoping for) a script assignment or staff writing job, though I trust you would recover from the thunderbolt of such an offer quickly enough to accept it on the spot.

Just get in the door. Take *any* job in the industry. Then let your talent and desire do the rest.

Computer Skills...Hey, It's The '90s!

The most desirable entry-level position is that of a *writers' assistant.* If you are lucky enough to land such a job, you will be able to watch, listen, learn and win the affection and loyalty of the writers for whom you are working outlandish hours for starvation wages.

Writers' assistant jobs require an absolute mastery of computers and word processing software, skills I submit you will need anyway. I used to write in black ink on yellow legal pads (and still do for first drafts of dialogue), but the computer has changed my working life. The only machine that ever meant more to me was my first washing machine.

If *I* can develop computer skills, there is hope for anyone, and if you are trying to get in the door of a production office, it's a skill you'd better have. In the past four years, I have had two young writers as assistants. Both were incredibly hard-working, accommodating, cheerful, and funny computer whizzes. And both are now working television writers.

Television is one of the most powerful influences—good *and* bad—in contemporary society. It harbors any number of people, including writers, who are there solely for the money and to give the audience what they think the audience wants.

But it is also the working arena for a wide variety of creative, thoughtful, positive individuals who have important things to say about the human condition, and who understand the responsibilities inherent in providing product for mass entertainment.

There is a place out there for young people with energy and talent and the desire to do good work.

There is a place out there for *you.*

If you want to claim your place, persevere.

CLAIRE LABINE was a staff writer on "Captain Kangaroo," co-head writer of "Where The Heart Is" and "Love of Life" (CBS-TV), co-creator, executive producer, and headwriter of "Ryan's Hope" (ABC-TV), and writer of various movies of the week.

She has eight Emmies and twelve Writer's Guild of America awards.

7

Writing The "Unwritten" Shows

Joseph W. Scher, President, Writer/Producer
Joseph Scher Productions

It's been my good fortune (or misfortune) to write some TV shows that no one thinks are written. I'm talking about such staples as "Macy's Thanksgiving Day Parade Show," "The Orange Bowl Parade Show"...yes, even "The Miss America Pageant." Viewers assume shows like these just *happen*. That they're events, almost like a live news break. How in the world do you "write" something like that?

Well, the toughest part of the job probably is being asked to write it in the first place. This usually happens when the producer is unhappy with his last writer and is desperately seeking a replacement. How the producer comes to choose you can be a quirky thing. I was asked to write my first "Thanksgiving Day Parade Show" because of a recommendation to the producer by the lighting director of another show I had worked on. You never know who's watching you.

Getting Ready To Write

OK, you've got the assignment. Now what? The thing about a parade show that is so deceptive is it all seems ad-libbed. Don't those charming hosts just make up all those witty comments as they go along? They usually don't. The writer does.

Perhaps a month before the day of the parade, the producer puts together a "line-up"—a listing of every element in the parade (bands, floats, guest stars, balloons, etc.) in the order in which they will appear. He gives the line-up to the writer along with the background information on the various participants. And he says: "I need the script in three weeks. Go write." With that stirring command ringing in your ears, you slink off to your typewriter or computer. (I'm a recent convert to a word processing IBM compatible. All my old scripts were rapped out on my still reliable Selectric II.)

As the writer (there's only one) on the "Thanksgiving Day Parade Show," you have the thrill of visiting the workshop and warehouse in Jersey City where all the intricate floats are designed and constructed. It helps to see in person the things you are going to be writing about. Unfortunately, you never get to sit down with the celebrities who will host the parade until after the script is written.

So there you are in your cluttered office with all the materials needed to put together the script—your notes, background information you've obtained, and your imagination. (NBC gave me an office at 30 Rockefeller Plaza in New York, but I prefer to write in *my* "international headquarters"—my office at home.)

Putting Words In Their Mouths

A writer plays all the parts. I suppose it helps if you're a split personality, like Sybil. First, you imagine you're Ed McMahon, the host welcoming the audience. The next minute you're Helen Reddy, or David Hartman or Della Reese or whomever else you're writing for. You try to imagine what would be appropriate for them to say as the parade passes by. And you write it, keeping it brief, witty and informative. You have to write something for every single element in the parade—more than a hundred different items. You also have to write "the upcomings,"—those little hypes before the commercials: "Coming up next, Dolly Parton, Mickey Mouse, and the United States Naval Academy Band. Don't go away."

And so it goes. Sitting at your lonely desk, fantasizing the whole parade before your eyes, jumping in and out of character as you write for the different personalities who will be broadcasting your script to millions across the nation.

The Words Come Alive

As the broadcast date nears, the producer schedules a production meeting with the cast, the musical director and you, the writer. This is the moment of truth—when you hear your lines read aloud by the talent. Now you get a feeling for whether or not the dialogue will "play." Sometimes you have to explain to the talent just how a line was meant to be read, or exactly what it means. If you have to explain it, it's usually not too good. So you re-write. And you re-write. And re-write.

On the day of the telecast, you are at the mercy of the host and hostess. Some will read the script as written. Once in a while you have a personality who thinks he can ad-lib his way through. In that lies disaster, because it can throw off all the timings. But, then, who really listens to the commentary anyway? Probably just the writer—and his wife. Besides, if the writer has done his job well, it will all sound like the hosts made it up on the spot. The audience will never think someone actually spent many hours writing the parade commentary.

In the end, there are two joys in writing an "unwritten" show like this—your name in the credits at the end of the program...and the paycheck.

Writing For Fun And Profit

Think you want to be a TV writer? Journalism is an excellent training ground (it worked for me), along with an interest in drama, music, cinema and everything else in the world. A writer has to know everything about everything—or at least know where to find it. If you've got the talent and the perseverance, with a little luck (and the right contacts), you'll make it.

How do you meet the right contacts?

I'm still working on that. I'll let you know.

JOSEPH SCHER has been a freelance TV and film writer for more than 20 years. He started his writing career as a television copywriter for three of the largest advertising agencies in New York—McCann-Erickson, Ted Bates (now Backer, Spielvogel, Bates) and BBD&O.

Since going on his own, he's written more than 50 television shows and numerous industrial and educational productions. His network credits include "The Miss America Pageant" (5 years); "Macy's Thanksgiving Day Parade Show" (3 years); "The Orange Bowl Parade Show;" "Salute To Sir Lew, The Master Showman," ABC-TV Special; and 44 episodes of the syndicated sports show, "Outdoors With Liberty Mutual." Clients for whom he's written films or videos include: IBM, Exxon, AT&T, Bristol-Myers Squibb, Schering-Plough, Merck, Thomas & Betts and many others.

During the past few years, Scher has added the titles of producer and director to his business card. He operates out of his home in Scotch Plains, New Jersey.

8

Careers In Cable Television

National Cable Television Association

The cable television boom is here to stay. What started as a means of improving poor television reception in rural areas has developed into an industry providing a myriad of exciting technologies and viewing options that have dramatically changed the course of telecommunications.

To simplify the technical explanation of how cable works: It uses antennas constructed on high ground to pick up signals from broadcast airwaves, microwave transmitters, or satellites, delivers them to a "headend" site, then transmits them to the home through a coaxial cable and/or optical fiber network. This "closed path" allows households that couldn't receive over-the-air transmissions to receive television—and more channels than they ever dreamed of!

Cable television offers something for virtually everyone. Viewers can choose from a rich and diverse menu of programming and information options. As part of their basic cable service, viewers can be entertained by local talents and keep apprised of community developments through local programming channels. For the information-hungry viewer, cable offers everything from around-the-clock news to college credit courses. In addition, cable is now the home of the finest in film, comedy, sports, music and documentary programming.

Not surprisingly, cable has become so popular that it now serves nearly 60 percent of all American television households—a number that continues to grow every day.

Rapid Growth Means Expanding Opportunities

As a result of the industry's rapid growth, numerous exciting employment opportunities exist in the cable TV business. Since 1975, the industry workforce has more than tripled in size—from 25,000 to over 91,000 full-time employees. This number will continue to increase as systems are rebuilt and upgraded, and programming becomes even more sophisticated and diverse.

Along with the rapid development of cable television's workforce has come a very clear commitment to Equal Employment Opportunities (EEO). The Cable Communications Policy Act of

1984—the main regulatory legislation for the industry—sets out specific guidelines for all cable systems to ensure equal opportunity in employment throughout the industry. Cable entities must also comply with regulations adopted by the Federal Communications Commission specifically for the cable industry.

Promising career opportunities in this rapidly evolving industry will be available in the 1990s and beyond. Whether you are interested in business, technology, television production or a host of other fields, there is likely to be a place for you within one of the three types of organizations that serve as cable's primary employers:

- **Local Cable Systems**—which directly provide cable TV service to your home and community.
- **Multiple System Operators (MSOs)**—corporate entities composed of just a few to more than one hundred individual cable systems.
- **Cable Networks**—program networks which provide the programming found on each channel offered by the cable system.

This article is intended to give a general description of the types of positions that exist in each of the three segments of the cable industry. While job qualifications and responsibilities are listed for each position described, it is important to note that these are for general purposes and will certainly vary from region to region, city to city.

Career Opportunities With Cable Systems

It's the local cable system's job to provide subscribing customers with a clear, uninterrupted television signal delivered directly to the home via cable. To accomplish this goal, the local cable system typically requires the combined efforts of a variety of skilled persons. In smaller systems, however, one person may handle more than one of these functions:

- The *system management* will oversee all aspects of the operation listed below. The size of the management team and duties of individual managers will vary according to the size of the system.
- The *technical* staff maintains the cable wires, or plant, by performing installations, completing repair work, responding to problems arising at the customer's home, and developing and implementing new services.
- The *administrative* staff coordinates the activity of the technical staff and handles payments, billing and other customer needs.
- The *marketing, public relations and advertising* staff works to project a positive public image of cable programming and the cable system to the community, and to generate increased revenue through the subscription and advertising sales.
- The *programming and production* staff creates locally originated programs and assists the community with local access programming.

The by-words of this consumer-oriented business are customer satisfaction. All areas in the company are interrelated and focus on providing quality service and diverse viewing options to the community.

Management

The *general manager*—head of the cable system office—is responsible for conducting the operational affairs of the system, interpreting and applying the policies of corporate management, and coordinating all functions of the system. All department heads will generally report to him or her. Qualifications for this position will usually include a college degree in Business Administration with industrial management experience.

Technical

The top position in the technical department is the *chief engineer*, which requires superior management skills and first-rate technical knowledge. The chief engineer is responsible for all technical concepts of cable system design, equipment planning, layout for cable communications service, specification of standards for equipment and material, construction of facilities, equipment installation, and technical advice and counsel to the various staff and system operating managers. Qualifications for the position include a degree in Electrical Engineering or equivalent experience.

The most highly skilled of the technical staff is the *chief technician*. As the supervisor of all technicians, he or she normally does not work in the field, but may be required to do so when complex problems arise. Qualifications for this position include an industrial background and electronic training plus extensive "hands-on" experience.

Technical staff: The *trunk technician* is called upon to correct any electronic failures in the main line or the feeder amplifier. The *service technician* responds to problems with a subscriber's cable reception, which often requires service calls to the home (though the service technician also works on the amplifiers, poles and lines). The *bench technician* operates the cable system's repair facility. Broken or malfunctioning equipment are brought to the repair facility for examination, where this technician must diagnose the problem, repair it, record the repair and return the malfunctioning piece to use if possible. Because the actual analysis and repair is completed by this technician, the position requires a strong electronics background. Qualifications for the positions of trunk, service, and bench technicians include some electronics training.

Generally, the first step on a cable technician's career ladder is the position of *installer*. An installer prepares the customer's home for cable reception, which may require running a cable wire from a utility pole to a television set. Qualifications for the position of installer include some trade school with demonstrated mechanical aptitude.

Administration

- *Office Manager*—experience in office administration and personnel management.
- *Customer Service Representative (CSR), Service Dispatcher*—high school diploma and good communications skills.
- *Accounts Payable Clerk, Accounts Receivable Clerk, Billing Clerk*—two years of college with a strong bookkeeping and business background.

Marketing, Public Affairs, And Advertising

The *public affairs director* serves as a liaison between the cable system and the local government and community which it serves. This job may include working with local government officials who monitor the local cable franchise, meeting with civic groups to discuss cable programming and service, organizing projects and events to help support the community, and alerting the local media to progress and changes within the cable system.

The *marketing director* is responsible for increasing the number of subscribers to the cable system. He or she develops and coordinates all marketing activity by creating promotional programs, overseeing market research, and supervising advertising to ensure public acceptance of services and products. Qualifications for the positions of public affairs director and marketing director include a degree in Public Relations or Marketing and related experience.

The *researcher* must determine community needs by conducting demographic studies of the area. Research studies are also utilized in the expansion of an existing system, determining saturation rates, and identifying additional programming needs. For the analytical or detail-oriented person, this is an area worth examining. Qualifications for the position of researcher include a degree in marketing.

Once research is completed and promotional packages prepared, the system's cable services must be sold to the public. *Sales representatives* conduct house-to-house calls and contact managers of hotels and apartment complexes to inform them of the benefits of cable TV. To complement the door-to-door drive, direct mail campaigns are also conducted, and the sales staff has input into the creation and implementation of promotional sales ideas. Many cable systems employ *telemarketing sales representatives* who call both non-subscribers and subscribers to sell cable services. Qualifications for a position on the sales staff include a high school diploma with some sales experience.

The *advertising sales team* must market the cable system as a viable advertising medium for products and services. The sales team will usually deal directly with local merchants, while national and international manufacturers are usually contacted through advertising agencies or representatives. Qualifications for a position in advertising sales include some college or a public relations, advertising or sales background.

Programming And Production

The *director of local origination* is responsible for creating and coordinating community programming. This person supervises all phases of a local production, from conceiving the program to writing the scripts and overseeing the technical production.

The *director of public access* is responsible for the operation of cable channels made available for use by the public. A community education campaign may be conducted by the director to acquaint the public with the availability and operation of this service.

Qualifications for the positions of director of local origination and director of public access include degrees in Communications and hands-on experience in production.

When a cable system produces its own programming, a staff is usually necessary for production. The responsibilities of a *producer* vary depending on the size of the studio facilities, but he or she usually selects the cast and schedules the day-to-day rehearsals and taping sessions. The producer (who may even write the script) makes all decisions concerning camera shots, angles and choice of cameras used during actual production.

When the script is written and the visual interpretation prepared, it is the job of the *assistant director* to prepare the studio for production. This entails properly placing and checking equipment, coordinating timing with the camera crew, acting as a liaison between the director and technical crew during production, and working the video control board.

Qualifications for the positions of producer and assistant director include a degree in Communications and moderate to extensive experience in production.

The *audio technician* is responsible for timing musical cues and monitoring all sound effects and dialogue for pitch and volume. The *lighting technician* is responsible for reinforcing the mood and atmosphere of a production by creating special effects through lighting. During a production, the *floor manager* is in contact with the control room. He or she aids in camera cues and provides silent signals to the cast. After completion of the filming or taping, the *editor*, under the supervision of the producer, electronically splices the tape and produces the program in its final form. The *studio technician* is responsible for the overall technical management of the studio. This technician will purchase and repair equipment, diagnose problems, and assure that the facility is operational.

Qualifications for the positions of audio and lighting technicians, floor manager, editor and studio technician include an electronics background and hands-on experience in the respective fields.

Career Opportunities With Multiple System Operators (MSOs)

In addition to a number of individually-owned cable systems throughout America, nearly 900 corporate and regional businesses own and operate more than one cable system. These companies, which own anywhere from a few to several hundred systems, are called multiple system operators (MSOs).

The personnel structure within the MSO headquarters or regional offices often closely mirrors that of individual cable systems. However, while the primary function of a cable system is to bring cable TV to subscribers, the purpose of the MSO is to provide support services to these cable systems or field offices. For instance, by virtue of volume, an MSO may be capable of receiving greater discounts on equipment and supplies, and thus could serve as the purchasing agent for its systems. Additionally, MSOs typically develop budgets, maintain Federal Communications Commission (FCC) records, and explore new business opportunities for their systems.

Operations Management

The *vice president of operations management* is typically assisted by the following directors:

- *Director of management information services*—responsible for overseeing all data processing, system analysis and software programming.
- *Director of training*—assists other MSO employees in developing necessary technical, managerial and personal skills.
- *Regional managers*—act as liaisons between the MSO and the individual cable systems, implementing corporate strategies and operational policies.

Qualifications for positions within the operations management department include degrees in Business Administration and related system experience.

Sales & Marketing

The following people report to the *vice president of sales and marketing:*

- *Director of ad sales*—solicits advertising at the national level.
- *Director of telemarketing*—oversees telephone surveys of subscribers and potential system subscribers.
- *Director of marketing*—makes programming decisions based on advertising, telemarketing and research information.
- *Director of marketing research*—monitors consumer trends and program preferences, testing the effectiveness of promotional efforts and program scheduling.

Qualifications for positions within the sales and marketing department include a degree in Business and Marketing and related experience.

Public Affairs

The *vice president of public affairs* coordinates information between the MSO and member cable systems, the media, consumers and the government. Assistance in these efforts is provided by:

- *Regional public affairs directors*—handle the management of public affairs for their assigned regions, and serve as liaisons between the system public affairs directors and the MSO vice president.
- *Director of government affairs*—establishes and maintains contact with public officials and regulatory agencies by providing them with information about the cable company, representing the corporation at hearings and other meetings, and monitoring legislation and other regulatory matters.

Qualifications for positions within the public affairs department include a degree in Communications and related experience.

Human Resources

The *vice president of human resources* is assisted by the *director of personnel* in complying with the Equal Employment Opportunity (EEO) standards in hiring personnel, establishing compensation and benefits packages, and managing staff development and employee relations. Qualifications for positions within the human resources department include a degree in Business Administration and related experience.

Finance

Expenses and revenues for each of the individual cable systems must be balanced and transcribed by the MSO into appropriate documents for the FCC, lending institutions and investors. It is the responsibility of the *vice president of finance* to determine strategy and make policy decisions for all of the MSO's member systems based on the "bottom line" calculated by the following individuals:

- *Director of accounting*—balances the accounts and reports the financial status of the member systems, as well as those of the MSO.
- *Director of corporate development*—explores investment opportunities and develops expansion strategies.

Qualifications for positions within the finance department include advanced degrees in Finance or Accounting and extensive related experience.

Career Opportunities With Cable Programming Networks

Perhaps the fastest growing aspect of cable television today is production and programming. Since 1975, when Home Box Office (HBO) first utilized satellite technology to transmit programming nationwide, over 100 national and regional cable programming networks have been launched.

There are several types of cable programming networks:

- **Basic Cable Networks**—advertiser-supported to some degree, and generally available with a combination of other basic networks for a fixed monthly subscription fee.
- **Pay-TV Networks**—predominantly all-movie or all-sports channels, often shown without commercial interruption and available as an addition to the basic package for a monthly fee.
- **Pay-Per-View**—event programming (i.e., boxing, concerts) or movies that can be bought on an individual basis.

Programming

The *programming executive's* responsibilities may include determining the appropriate mix and scheduling of programs, negotiating purchases of movies or syndicated programs, managing in-house productions, coordinating programming contracted to independent production companies, and supervising staff within the programming department.

Producers, assistant directors, audio technicians, lighting technicians, floor managers, editors, and *studio technicians* are likely to be employed by cable networks, typically in greater numbers than by cable systems. Additionally, those networks that produce original news programs require *researchers* to investigate and prepare news reports. For networks that produce talk shows or entertainment programs, *talent bookers* may be employed. Qualifications for the position of researcher include a degree in Journalism. Qualifications for the position of talent booker include related experience.

Sales

At a basic cable network, the *vice president of ad sales, regional directors* and *account executives* are responsible for contracting advertisers to purchase air time nationwide. At the Music Television Channel (MTV), for instance, that may mean selling commercial spots to Ronco Records to promote a special album collection.

The *affiliate relations department* is set up much like the ad sales department, but the "product" for sale is the network and the "pitch" is made to two distinct audiences: cable systems and cable subscribers. An example of this would be an agreement between Showtime and Pizza Hut to include subscription reduction coupons in every pizza box.

Qualifications for positions within the ad sales and affiliate relations department include degrees in Business, Marketing, or Communications, and related sales experience.

Communications

The print medium still reigns as the chief source of criticism in the entertainment world, and therefore, it is the job of the *communications director* to promote the network to consumer and trade writers assigned to cover television. For instance, the communications director may send preview tapes of certain programs to a TV writer for a major daily newspaper to try to win a favorable review. Or, statistics about the increasing number of affiliates carrying the network may be sent to popular trade magazines within the television industry.

Qualifications for the position of communications director include a degree in Communications or Journalism and experience in public relations or a related field.

Education

All technical jobs in cable usually require some special training. Although schools specializing in this field are limited, the cable industry is beginning to meet its own demand for trained technical personnel by providing more on-the-job training and special training schools. Community agencies and education systems are also developing technical training schools for cable communications. A Bachelor's and Master's degree in Engineering is necessary for highly technical positions in cable systems and at corporate headquarters.

Non-technical positions usually require additional training and education. A Bachelor's degree in Business Administration can provide entry into several areas. This degree requires four years of study with a concentration in marketing, advertising, finance, or general business administration. A Bachelor's degree in Telecommunications or Communications also requires a four-year course of study. After basic courses are taken, the student can specialize in journalism, radio and television, or communications media.

Many community colleges offer an Associate degree in both Business Administration and Communications. These degrees involve two years of course work in specific areas of concentration and usually include some hands-on experience.

The Job Search

If you are interested in pursuing a career in the cable television industry, there are many places where you may begin your job search:

- Contact cable systems in your geographic area. If your local telephone directory does not list them under "Television—Cable," you can consult the *TV Factbook* published by Television Digest, which lists by state all cable systems in the United States and Canada. This two-volume publication should be available at your local library.
- Contact local government officials to find out the status of cable service in your area.
- Refer to the industry trade publications in Appendix B. These may also be available in the local library.
- Contact the state or regional cable association in your area for further information on system locations and activities. These associations are generally located in the state's capital city.
- Contact someone you know who works, or has worked, within the industry for information on job openings.
- Contact one of the cable professional associations listed in Appendix A.
- Contact one of the MSOs or programming networks.
- Watch for cable representatives at high school and college job fairs.
- Ask your local cable system about internship programs that may be offered to students interested in entering the cable industry.

When conducting your job search, don't fail to examine industries related to cable television. These industries include: equipment suppliers, financial institutions, marketing and advertising agencies, and programming services.

There are as many doors in as there are people interested!

The **NATIONAL CABLE TELEVISION ASSOCIATION** (NCTA) is the major trade association of the nation's cable system owners and operators, programmers and manufacturers.

9

Evaluating A Career In Corporate Television

Tom McCabe
Freelance Producer, Director & Editor

There is certainly no question that in less than half a century, television has become the predominant means by which people receive information and entertainment. It is the medium that virtually everyone has seen, recognizes, and will respond to. For that reason, many large organizations—major corporations, nonprofits like the Red Cross, and government agencies— have established internal video production departments as key parts of their communications efforts.

Is it a career field worth considering? Can you switch to broadcast television? What's the difference between the television we watch at home and "corporate" television? Is there enough stability in corporate television to make it viable career option? What skills will be required to be successful in the future?

In many cases, these questions will have to be answered on an individual basis. But there are some benefits and drawbacks to corporate television I can share with you.

Let's Take A Closer Look

There are many different ways in which a video ("corporate television") department can be integrated into an organization. It may be in a communications, marketing, or education division; whatever programs are developed will reflect the orientation of the division in which it *is* included. Typical programs produced include staff training tapes, product sales and demonstration videos, and in-house news or information programs.

Corporate television or, in a broader context, non-broadcast television, is, in most ways, very similar to broadcast and entertainment television. The same basic tools and techniques are used, the jargon is the same, and the skills required are similar.

A corporate facility can be as small as a one-man shop or big enough to include one hundred or more producers, directors, editors and technicians. Many of the Fortune 100 companies, in fact, have video departments that rival major production houses in size, budget and skill.

Outside this select 100, the size of corporate video departments can vary widely, though they typically are made up of five to a dozen people, most of whom are producers. Producers are the people that are *responsible* for the production and completion of video programs, whether or not they do the actual work themselves.

Many corporations have very little video production equipment of their own. In this case, it is the producer's job to assign the tasks of writing, shooting, and editing a program to freelance people or production companies. He or she might also write a script, rent equipment to shoot with, and then arrange to edit the program at a local post-production facility.

The Pros...

An advantage for entry-level personnel in the corporate world is that the path to becoming a key part of the production team or a producer is usually much quicker in a corporate facility than it might be in a production company, ad agency or network affiliate. In addition, it offers an opportunity to combine an interest in video production with interest or expertise in another area. For example, a budding producer that is also a runner might be able to find a job with an athletic shoe company's video department.

The reverse is also true: Producing a video program on a given topic may require a fair amount of management skill and in-depth knowledge of the subject to make a successful program. A number of corporate video personnel have gone on to become vice presidents of marketing or some other high-level, non-video title in the same company.

Producing in a corporation also offers a great deal of creative control. As one of the few video experts in the organization, clients have to rely on your ideas and expertise to make a program work. By contrast, people working for a production company or ad agency may have to sell their ideas to dozens of TV people, each with a different vision of the finished product and a plethora of suggestions about how to achieve it.

...And Cons

There are, of course, some disadvantages to corporate television. Corporate TV lacks the glamour of broadcast TV. Job security is related to company strength, not ratings or video sales. But because video production is rarely central to the operation of a company or organization, it may be one of the first departments to be trimmed or eliminated during lean times.

In addition, the high cost of video gear means that only a few large or heavily committed companies are willing to spend large sums on high-end or state-of-the-art video production equipment. Working with the latest and greatest video gear is usually limited to people working for very large corporations or production companies.

Realistically, of course, some programs can also be pretty dry. Producing a one-hour training program on how to operate industrial incinerators may make working for the lowliest local cable show eminently attractive by comparison.

A Typical Operation

As the manager of a video facility at Applied Data Research, a software company, I was responsible for coordinating the activities of a video department that worked closely with three other departments within the Marketing Communications Division, whose job was primarily to support the company's marketing and sales efforts. The four departments included slide production, print production, video production (my area), and writers (for print and video).

The four department managers would meet once a week with the Director of Marketing Communications to discuss projects and coordinate activities. The video group consisted of three producers, one of whom was a manager, a technician, *and* a video engineer. All members of the staff could shoot and edit video programs, although skill levels varied.

Often a brochure promoting a new software product would be produced in tandem with a sales "video" and a 35mm slide presentation. Salesmen would carry the package into the field as a sales kit to promote products. Others projects included the production of training programs for new salesmen, and the production of a monthly company video news magazine. Although unusual for a company of our size, all shooting and editing was done in-house.

Although officially a "nine-to-five" job, strict deadlines meant occasional late nights for everyone.

Salaries at our company ranged from $18,000 for the technician (an entry-level position) to $40,000 for senior producer.

Where The Jobs Are...And How To Get One

Because most corporate video departments are part of or closely situated to company or organizational headquarters, jobs in this area are located, for the most part, in large metropolitan areas.

By far the best way to land an entry-level job is as an intern. An internship gives newcomers a sense of the kind of work being performed and a feel for personnel needs within an organization. Some corporations that do not have formal intern programs can be sold on creating one if it is kept simple. *(The most complete listing of available internships is included in a brand-new Career Press publication—Interships, Volume 5: Radio & Television, Broadcasting & Production—Ed.)*

Occasional entry-level openings for production assistants, junior editors, or technicians are advertised in large newspapers and trade magazines. But don't think "entry-level" means "no experience." Solid hands-on equipment experience is a *must*—most entry-level positions include running tape machines and cameras as primary functions.

A college degree is usually required for writing or producing jobs.

A solid short (5 minute) demo reel with the applicant's role clearly defined is nearly always required.

The Future

For many years, corporate television has typically been a small-scale version of broadcast and entertainment television. Finished programs would be completed in a linear fashion for distribution, usually onto a small format videotape such as VHS.

There are a number of developing trends, however, that may make for dramatic changes between corporate and broadcast TV. The use of television for two-way video teleconferencing, for example, is becoming a popular way to connect large, geographically diverse organizations.

New technologies, particularly computers, are using video as a component of some other medium, such as computer graphics or videodiscs. As a result, future sales and training programs may combine photographs, computer graphics, and video into a single presentation.

TV production equipment continues to offer more and more powerful tools targeted specifically for the low-end user. In years to come, this could well mean that production skills between corporate and broadcast TV will not be as readily interchangeable as today.

So those of you entering corporate television may need to be even more certain that it is the career track you want to pursue, not just an experience you hope to use as a training ground and steppingstone to a broadcast television career.

TOM MCCABE has been writing, producing and directing video programs for industry and broadcast since 1979.

Prior to becoming a freelance producer, director and editor in 1988, he was the manager of the Television Production Center at Applied Data Research for four years. Based in Princeton, New Jersey, he works primarily for corporate clients such as AT&T, Hewlett-Packard, Schering-Plough, Veterinary Learning Systems, the United States Tennis Association and others.

Tom has associate degrees in communications, photography, and avionics technology.

The **INTERNATIONAL TELEVISION ASSOCIATION** (ITVA) is the umbrella group under which non-broadcast television producers and users share information. It offers a number of valuable services for members including a magazine and newsletter that follow industry trends, an annual salary survey, a job hotline, and other member services. Student memberships are available at a reduced rate. Information on local chapters and membership can be obtained from ITVA, 6311 N. O'Connor Road, LB-51, Irving, TX 75039.

10

A Quick Take On
Corporate Video Production

Timothy Sheahan, Producer/Director
Sheahan Productions, Inc.

While you're out looking for work in video, don't overlook one of the fastest growing areas of video production—corporate video. Corporate video is rapidly expanding and provides many production and management opportunities for graduates in video.

*(This is the second article on corporate television in this **Career Directory**—the other is by freelance producer Tom McCabe. Though both articles ostensibly cover the same topic, we thought they were different enough—and offered enough different advice—to include both—The Editors.)*

Most corporations are involved in video in some way, and are using the medium for many communication applications, including marketing and sales presentations, interactive video for training, live shows broadcast via satellite to locations throughout the world, teleconferencing, and many others.

The production of these programs is usually managed in one of two ways: either the corporation has an in-house fully-staffed department, or they hire independent producers or production companies.

The in-house video department can range in size depending on the volume of video produced and the size of the corporation. It can be a small, one-person operation with no equipment or facilities that relies on outside facilities and crews to help put a program together. Or, it can be a staff of 30 people, including producers, directors, writers, camerapersons, editors, etc., complete with a large studio with full production capabilities.

The Role Of The Corporate Video Producer

In either case, the role of the producer is essentially the same. The producer is responsible for overseeing the entire project from concept to completion. This includes getting the project produced on schedule and within budget, and the hiring of all the resources—from make-up artist to video duplication facility—to complete the project.

The producer's role in the pre-production stage of a video project is to consult with the client, usually another executive within the corporation, such as a marketing or training manager. Initially, a meeting will be set up to discuss the viability of the project, ideas, budget and scheduling.

Once the video is "a go," the producer begins booking the individuals and facilities needed for the project. Set designers, graphic designers, camera crews, studios for both shooting and sound, editing facilities, and others all have to be contacted and scheduled.

In many cases, the producer is also a writer or a director. Many producers in corporate video have titles like "writer/producer" or "producer/director." Some write, produce *and* direct. Depending on the producer and the project, the producer may choose to handle all three functions, or just produce and then hire a writer or director.

The Day As A Corporate Producer

One of the reasons I love to produce video is the variety of projects, people, and new experiences I am exposed to in my work. Each day is different for me.

My last week is a good example. I was shooting physicians in Houston and Dallas for a major pharmaceutical company at the beginning of the week, and by the end of the week I was doing a sound mix in New York City for a major cookie and cracker manufacturer. Talk about diversity! Of course, there are also times when I'm in my office all day on the phone and doing paperwork.

How To Become A Corporate Producer

As with most staff positions within corporations, you'll need a college degree. I landed a job as an associate producer three months after graduating college. The reason for my success was simple—*I had hands-on experience!* Whatever you do, get some!

Be willing to work for free, *beg* if you have to. The hardest part is getting in, but once you do, you'll see how easy it is to find future work. And don't despair. If you find yourself hauling cables, typing labels and fetching coffee, hang in there. Your opportunity will come! Remember, you could be flipping burgers and doing nothing for your video career somewhere else.

You have to be aggressive (not obnoxious!) in turning up an opportunity. Call up corporate video departments, TV stations, cable companies, production companies, advertising agencies...anybody that is producing video. You need *any* hands-on experience, so don't limit yourself to a corporate video department. Ask them if they offer internships. If they don't, ask them if they'd like to *start* an internship program with you. If all else fails, ask if you can work for *free!*

Yes, free! One of my most valuable work experiences while I was a student was with Nike Sports Productions. I found out they had a new video production group, so I approached one of the producers and proposed that I be their production assistant, gofer, (whatever they wanted to call me!) for the summer. All he would have to do was fill out a performance review for my advisor at the end of the term. I not only received 15 college credits, but had some of the best hands-on experience I could ever get! To top it off, after I left the full-time internship, I was hired to work freelance on other jobs.

The moral of the story is, even though a formal internship program may not be established, don't let it stop you. Show people you are enthusiastic and willing to work hard, and you will go a long way.

Eventually, you will get paid. The salary range of corporate producers can start at $20,000 a year and go to $50,000-$60,000 per year. Salaries are always dependent upon experience, the region of the country you live in, and the company itself.

Where To Find The Jobs

Most opportunities will be found through word-of-mouth and video organizations. If you do search the newspapers, keep in mind that the job titles can vary from "producer," to "video specialist," "media production specialist," and "audiovisual producer."

One organization that is invaluable for getting contacts in corporate video, as well as for professional growth, is the International Television Association (ITVA). This organization is comprised of thousands of production executives—primarily in corporate video—and has local chapters all over the United States. I highly recommend getting involved and attending local meetings. You'll meet other professionals and stay on top of the industry with their seminars and informal meetings.

The ITVA also has a national job hotline for members that lists available positions throughout the U.S. For membership information, contact the ITVA national headquarters in Irving, Texas.

Most major cities also have local video/film organizations comprised of professionals in the business. Try to get involved with these groups and go to the meetings and seminars they offer. If they need volunteer help, by all means, sign up! This is a great way to make contacts and find opportunities.

Hang In There

Chances are you've already heard this a hundred times if you've begun your job search. Or maybe you've just been told how "competitive" the field is and that finding a job will be tough. That's true. However, if you are prepared, if you've done your homework, there's no reason you can't be just as competitive as the next person.

TIMOTHY SHEAHAN has been producing and directing videos for over ten years for a variety of major corporate clients.

Prior to starting his own company, he was a staff senior producer for Schering-Plough Corporation in New Jersey. Tim was also a staff producer for Creative Media Development, Inc., in Portland, Oregon. He has freelanced as an editor, cameraman, and photographer.

Tim has won numerous national industry awards as a producer/director. He holds a Bachelor's degree in Television and Film and a Master's degree in Instructional Technology from the University of Oregon. Tim currently resides in Princeton, New Jersey.

11

Becoming A Television Engineer— It Takes More Than Just Math!

Society of Motion Picture & Television Engineers

In commercial and public television stations all over the United States and Canada, engineers and technicians operate the broadcast and transmission installations that bring programs to home TV sets.

They are involved with arrangements for live programs originating in local or network studios, taped and filmed material, remote hook-ups of special events, and slides and graphic visuals.

In educational television, programs are transmitted live, or through tape or film, to the schools in a system or to a broadcast area.

In cable television systems, engineers and technicians monitor and maintain playback and transmission equipment. They must also help originate local programs, using film or video cameras.

A university, a hospital or an industry may have its own closed-circuit television system. In such a case, the television engineer may be responsible for designing and installing a television system which might be used for teaching surgical techniques, providing sports fans with instant replay of key action in a football game, or transmitting library reference material from a remote location.

Whatever the situation, whatever the purpose, there is a galaxy of complicated equipment to be installed, operated, monitored for quality, and maintained.

Television is a field in which development has been phenomenally rapid; yet there remain many unsolved problems offering possibilities for tremendous growth and challenge. Videotape recording, for example, greatly increased the flexibility of television. Engineers are now working to develop its untapped potential for home and school use.

Increasing demands by those who want to take advantage of television's power to inform, instruct and entertain will present problems not yet recognized by those who choose work in television as a career field.

Getting Ready For A Career

Preparation will vary with the area you choose and the kind of work you think will be most appropriate for you. A high school background in science, math, shop, mechanical drawing and photography is most advantageous.

Beginning Technicians

To this high school preparation, beginning technicians will add on-the-job training and, probably, vocational or technical school courses such as electronics, optics, machine shop, photography, and equipment maintenance and repair. Many community colleges offer technical and professional programs of special interest to the job-oriented person. Concentrated study focused on a specialty may be more appropriate to your goals than a traditional academic course at a four-year college or university.

Beginning Engineers

At the professional level, engineers need at least a Bachelor's degree. This will be supplemented with on-the-job training and experience working on assigned projects under supervision. Typical undergraduate majors are engineering, mathematics or the physical sciences, with specific courses pointing toward your field of interest.

Careers In Research

These require preparation beyond the Bachelor's degree and usually beyond the Master's degree for specialization in a chosen field.

Careers In Management And Administration

A professional-level science and engineering background is required, with preparation and experience in business and economics related to the photographic technologies and their applications.

Education Is Important

New equipment is constantly being devised, and new materials and procedures are developed very rapidly in response to problems and demands. You will have to study continually—either independently or in formal courses—to keep up with what is happening. Many companies encourage their employees to continue their education, and in some cases provide opportunities for them to do so by paying their expenses for advanced courses and degree programs.

Industry-wide studies have indicated that automation is becoming an increasingly significant factor, encompassing many of the mechanical operations. As this happens, the number and extent of routine jobs will decrease. However, machines will never replace judgement. The cameraman, the craftsman, the skilled printer—the creative person—will always be in demand. Equipment, materials and processes will become more complex, electronics increasingly important, and the general spectrum of photographic jobs more involved, necessitating a higher degree of basic education.

Where Are The Jobs?

This is a question which many ask, and rightly so. How many jobs are available at a particular time depends in part on the general state of the national economy and in part on the current demand for collection of information and communication of ideas in the specialty that interests you. Fields with especially strong growth rates at present include local television and instructional technology.

Hundreds of television stations and cable television systems across the United States and Canada require a growing number of technicians qualified to install, operate and maintain increasingly sophisticated broadcast and transmission equipment, as well as a growing number of film producers and of people responsible for photographic services.

Demand Is High

Larger school systems, colleges, and corporations are developing coordinated communications programs. Demands are growing for technicians and engineers to design and maintain multimedia systems, closed-circuit television systems and facilities for display of a broad range of visual and audio materials.

Film producers, film printing and processing laboratories and film service companies have a wide spectrum of jobs from the highly creative to highly technical engineering positions. Equipment and materials manufacturers are developing and making the tools used by all of the communications systems already reviewed.

Government and industry research organizations use motion pictures and television continually in many functions not connected directly to the better-known uses of the communications media. Photo technology as a career field offers great variety in what you may choose to do and where you may choose to work. Whether you find your place near home or far away, in this country or abroad, you'll be in on an exciting career which offers personal satisfactions, contributions to scientific and technical progress, and the expansion of knowledge in the world around us.

Initial Salaries

Starting salaries vary—as in any career—and they are affected by several factors—your abilities, preparation and experience, the type of job, "the job market" (the number of applicants per job), the location and the local cost of living. Advancement is influenced largely by your initiative, abilities and commitment to the field. If you're set on working in a particular part of the country or for a particular kind of employer, you may have to compromise on the matter of salary.

The jobs that brings with it the opportunity to grow and develop professionally is of particular importance. Even though the starting salary may be modest, in the long run it could well be the best paying job you can take.

In motion-picture production, many people work on a freelance basis and not in a regular year-round position. Pay is based on a daily rate. While this daily rate may seem extremely good, it is important to note that continuous employment is not guaranteed and you probably won't work full-time. It would be wise in this case to supplement your job with a related sales-oriented job.

Following Up

Your guidance counselor, advisor, or public library can help you locate additional information. Some perspective on the industry can be gained by looking through books and technical publications and the more general trade magazines.

Also, there may be people in your community who are involved in motion pictures or television—either directly or as clients of service companies. Local businesses and industries may use photographic or video techniques in research, training, manufacturing and marketing. Talk to people and become informed about the industry...you may just like what you see and hear.

SMPTE, The Society of Motion Picture and Television Engineers, was founded in 1916 to provide an opportunity for motion-picture and allied photographic engineers to exchange ideas and information and to stimulate technical progress primarily through standardization. Over the years, the scope of the Society has grown naturally to encompass the related fields of television, photoinstrumentation, and other areas of photographic science and engineering. Its objectives, however, are essentially unchanged:

- To provide an organization and a climate in which persons of like interests can meet, exchange ideas, and present technical papers for the advancement of, and education within, the spheres of interest of the Society;
- To provide a monthly technical journal for the publication of papers and the maintenance of a record of progress;
- To publish basic reference materials on specific technological problems important to the motion-picture and television industries;
- To establish standards and recommended practices that achieve the technological agreement of the industry, nationally and internationally;
- To provide guidance to students and to encourage high standards of education throughout the related disciplines; and
- To encourage the advancement of engineering technology and to sponsor lectures, exhibitions and conferences designed to advance the theory and practice of engineering within the scope of the Society.

A clearly defined interest in any phase of the industry is the principal requirement for membership in the SMPTE.

12

Lights, CAMERA, Action!

Anthony F. Pagano, President
Video Vision, Inc.

Lights, camera, action!

When you decide on a career as a cameraman, hearing these or similar words builds excitement as our blood pumps faster, our hands begin to perspire, and tension builds all around us.

Sound glamorous?

It is. But to reach that point in this business, we all have had to pay our dues. Hard work comes before all that glamor!

One Step At A Time

The title of *cameraman* takes time to achieve. To reach it, in most companies you must start at the bottom, often in a position titled *production assistant* (PA). When hired as a PA, you will learn what it takes to be a cameraman, but also be exposed to other areas of TV production. Production assistants are hired to drop cables, set up tripods and cameras, and assist the crew in whatever they require. You may also be asked to get coffee, food, etc. This less-than-glamorous position will give you an overall insight as to what it takes to make a production a complete success.

Common Sense And Mind Reading

Cameramen do not only zoom, pan, tilt, dolly or truck. They must interpret what the director has in mind for a particular shot. They must be able to take it upon themselves to get the shot as soon as possible without asking, "Is this okay," or "Do you want me to zoom closer?" When the director calls a command to a cameraman, he expects that the person on the camera is well-trained, has knowledge of his or her particular camera model, and is a self-motivated individual with a good amount of common sense. The cameraman must be able to make his camera operate smoothly and quickly.

Eyes And Ears Open

One of the best pieces of advice that I can offer anyone who wants to establish him- or herself in this industry is this: no matter what position you may be hired into, keep your eyes and ears open to everything that is going on around you. You will learn more by listening to years of experience (even if you totally don't agree), than any classroom can offer. You will learn short cuts that may not be what you were taught, but work! Just continue to listen and learn.

If you would like to express your comments regarding a production, I would recommend that you do this during a break or some other opportune time. Take the person responsible for the decisions aside from the others and talk to him or her privately. I can assure you by blurting out your ideas when you are not involved will cause nothing but heartaches for you. It's not that your ideas are not valid, but there is a time and a place for hearing *anything* from the "new kid on the block."

Part of your job could possibly involve travel and long hours. As glamorous as it sounds, this is one aspect of our profession that takes its toll on our health and personal life. I would safely say that sleep will win out over the excitement of a new city.

Starting Out

If you're set on becoming a cameraman, most high schools have programs that will give you an excellent foundation. Students have the opportunity to obtain extensive experience in camera operation, lighting, audio, set design, etc.

In college, communications will be your target, so take as many courses relating to the field you desire to enter. During the summers, you can get internships at major networks (NBC, CBS, ABC, etc.) or local cable companies. Your guidance counselor or school should have this information available to you. (You should also check *Internships, Vol. 5: Television & Radio, Broadcasting & Production,* published by Career Press, which lists internships at most of the biggest stations throughout the U.S. and Canada.) Check the phone book for local producers. They may not want someone full-time, but there is a chance they will need help with certain projects.

Just remember: learn all you can and always *keep your eyes and ears open.*

You must also decide if you want to freelance or work full-time. They both have their advantages and disadvantages, but I must say that there is stiff competition in the freelance market. On the positive side, when a producer/director likes your work, they are sure to call you back for more.

Keep in mind that if you decide to freelance, you become a business owner and need to provide your own health, car, and life insurance. You will, in fact, be responsible for all your own needs, including filing your taxes and selling your services.

I had a boss years ago who had a sign on his desk that read, "It's not how it is, it's how it looks." If you are going to run your own business, then do it right. If you look sloppy or unorganized, your client or director might assume that is also how you work. In this world of stiff competition, it pays to look good.

To Hold Or Not To Hold

The term cameraman is very vague. There are specialties within this category—some people, for example, are better in a studio than in the field, and vice versa.

There are experts in the art of handholding a camera. This may sound easy, but carrying around 20-30 pounds of camera equipment for a few hours has separated many men from the boys (sorry, ladies).

Some people like the excitement of ENG (Electronic News Gathering). Working on a news story is fast and furious. But remember: you carry the equipment and become the director's eyes and ears. The pressure is on from the time you leave the studio to the time you return. A good example was during the Gulf War when all the news media pointed their lenses to the skies to get that oh-so dramatic picture of a Patriot missle shooting down a Scud missile. A great majority of these shots are not just luck, but good planning.

On the other hand, working in a studio may sound dull to some, but hearing a live audience or "Here's Johnny" or working on a soap opera can be very exciting.

"I Made It"

Your day has finally arrived. You paid your dues, you've listened and learned, you fit into the routine. Now it's time for work. You can expect to arrive at least an hour and a half before a shoot (crew call). Although your camera might be set up by an engineer, you will need to set it up to your own specifications and comfort.

You will work with the director as he or she blocks the shots for you to take. You and the director will go over the script and work on angles. You will find yourself rehearsing, rehearsing, and rehearsing.

Once you put on headsets and it is show time, all your thoughts and actions will be controlled by the director calling the show. If you have any questions, they should have already been asked.

Be prepared for a wide variety of personality types among producers and directors...good *and* bad. Just keep in mind they are under extreme pressure to *get the shot*, so they may forget their tempers.

Pay Day

When starting out, you will obviously not be quickly on the way to your first million. Salaries will be competitive wherever you work, and are often dependent on geographical location and cost of living.

Check with your local cable or broadcast companies—they may be able to answer the questions you have.

"That's a rap!"
Good luck.

ANTHONY F. PAGANO started Video Vision, Inc. in 1980. Prior to starting his own company, he spent 14 years with Eastern Airlines and has an extensive background in management and training. Anthony specializes in corporate communications. His client lists range from the medical field to electrical manufacturers.

13

Always In The Spotlight!

Richard Tilley, President
Circuit Lighting Inc.

A lighting technician is someone who is trained to illuminate a person or object to achieve a specific visual effect.

In what is quickly becoming a 24-hour-a-day culture, the need for lighting has rapidly expanded the possibilities for those who wish to pursue a career in this field. Considering that Thomas Edison invented the incandescent bulb only 110 years ago, the growth in this industry has been phenomenal.

What Is The Purpose Of Lighting?

There are many reasons why we use lighting. Generally, it is an attempt to enhance a subject and make it stand out.

Lighting for commercials is commonly used to make a product more appealing.

Special effects can be created for a rock concert or disco.

The movie industry depends on lighting to bring out colors or create a natural effect.

Decorative lighting is being used more and more on a number of major buildings, hotels and monuments throughout the world. Used correctly, it can attract attention to a building or, in some cases, only highlight the attractive parts of a structure.

We're Not Just Talking Light Bulbs Here...

Professional lights are known as *fixtures* or *instruments*, of which there are numerous types. Light bulbs are known as *lamps* such as incandescent, fluorescent, quartz, and gas filled.

Lamps are contained in *fixtures*, which may be positioned in various configurations and controlled by people working with today's advanced technology. State-of-the-art technology offers computerized movement and positioning of fixtures. *Control consoles*—also known as *lighting boards* or *lighting switchboards*—may be either manual or automated.

There are many types of fixtures on the market, from the basic lamp holders that are commonly found in homes to high powered search lights. HMI, quartz, and incandescent fixtures are commonly used in theatre and television. Commercial fixtures such as ellipsoidals, fresnels, moles, and pars have a wide range of uses from theatrical events to concert lighting.

What Requires Artistic Lighting?

Many objects and people require artistic lighting. Here are a few examples:

1. *Background scenery* such as a building in the distance, a stage set, a group of people, or almost anything behind the object or person to be illuminated can be dramatically changed by the use of colored gel and dimmed lighting.

   If you had to light a group of people in a garden, for example, it would be possible—with the right lighting and gel—to just highlight certain areas or to completely change the color of the trees and flowers.

2. The *setting* must also be lit. Using the same group of people and the same garden, the setting—a park bench, a lamp post, or the group itself —would be lit from at least two sides to avoid shadows and ensure good coverage.

3. Now that the trees in our background have been lit and their colors highlighted, and the group, bench and lamp post illuminated, we have to decide how to light our *subject*—a specific member of the group.

4. In some instances, like a rock concert, it may also be necessary to light the *audience*.

What Effects Lighting Choices?

Economics

Many variables can affect the choices in lighting, but the most common is money. When a director or producer calls up a lighting company, what he or she wants invariably would cost far more than he or she has budgeted for lighting! So the very first questions will concern how to do the job the producer wants with the money in the budget...and where "creative solutions" can save money without significantly decreasing the desired lighting effects.

Space

The amount of space available will limit how much equipment can be brought into a room and, therefore, how complex the lighting effects can be.

Equipment Available

Not all lighting companies or studios have state-of-the-art equipment. Even the ones who do, may not have enough (or the right) equipment available at the time it is needed.

The Type Of Production

The type of production can dramatically change the kinds and amount of lights—video, for example, requires a different type of lighting than film.

Electricity Available

Without the use of generators, the average building only has a certain amount of electricity available—this alone can significantly effect the size and quantity of lights used.

The Market And The Consumers

The most abundant use of creative lighting is found in major metropolitan and large urban centers. New York, San Francisco, Los Angeles, Chicago, Boston, Miami, Orlando, Dallas, Fort Worth, and Houston are all cities where job opportunities are promising, but the market is not limited to these places. The following is just a partial list of typical end-users of a lighting technicians' services:

- Theatre performances (plays, musicals, opera and dance)
- Musical performances (concerts)
- Television production
- Film making
- Video production
- Entertainment centers (hotels, nightclubs, restaurants, museums, and theme parks)
- Religious organizations
- Sports arenas
- Educational centers (schools, colleges, universities, and training facilities)
- Retail operations (malls, stores, fashion events)
- Corporate functions
- Security systems (architectural, landscaping, residential, commercial and municipal)
- Government property (bridges, monuments, and buildings)

Entering The Field

There is no hard-and-fast route to becoming a lighting technician. Pathways for entering the field are as numerous as the personalities it attracts. Some key requirements, however, are an interest in math, electrical circuitry, and electronics. Proficiency in math facilitates both power usage computations and cost estimates, both key components of any lighting job. Since much of the equipment used is not always state-of-the-art, the ability to repair, substitute, or just "make do" with what is on hand is enhanced by a sound understanding of electrical principles. Courses in math and science offered in high school and vocational technical programs provide a good foundation for work in the lighting field.

Successful lighting technicians possess not only an artistic flair, but the motivation to keep pace with a constantly changing marketplace—the need to stay abreast of the fast-paced technological improvements in lighting products, supplies, and equipment is an essential component of the job.

Getting Valuable Experience

A variety of apprenticeships are available. Time spent as an electrician's helper or as a participant in a theatre group is valuable in determining latent ability and depth of interest in the field. Almost all schools and colleges stage annual theatre productions, and many communities support active theatre groups. The latter, however, are almost always understaffed and underbudgeted. As a result, they frequently welcome volunteers to share the work and are glad to share their knowledge in return.

Theatre production is generally divided into four segments: acting, costume and makeup, set building, and lighting. Of these, set building and lighting offer opportunities for hands-on learning that has served many technicians well.

What You Can Earn

Income is largely dependent upon the experience gained and parlayed into more complex lighting challenges that a designer will have to overcome. Earning potential is limited only by the experience and learning ability of the individual. Many apprentices earn between $30 and $75 a day, depending on prevailing economic conditions and the size and policies of the firm or organization they are working for. You will not get rich on these wages, but you should always include the value of the learning and experience as part of the pay.

While serving an average apprenticeship (usually lasting from 3 to 5 years), you will learn many different ways to light up a set, as well as a variety of "tricks of the trade." Although you may think that there's nothing left to learn after five years, it's good to remember that new products and ideas are common in this industry, and the equipment you have so patiently mastered could be obsolete...next week.

Once qualified and accepted into the lighting profession, it becomes easier to find work and to earn more when you do work. A freelance lighting technician on a tour or in the theatre can expect to earn up to $300 per day. Top-of-the-profession lighting directors collect fees in excess of several *thousand* dollars per day overseeing projects with million-dollar lighting budgets.

Most lighting technicians negotiate their income on an hourly, weekly, or per job basis. In addition, expense accounts and travel allowances are often available to cover cash outlays for food and housing while on the road.

Advancement Within The Industry

If you are creatively oriented, then your technical ability will be a sound foundation for fast advancement and job placement within the lighting design and fixture design industry. If you are a college graduate, then you could soon find yourself teaching others.

Freelance technicians usually work in the television and concert sides of the industry, since these usually don't require a full-time commitment and allow for greater flexibility.

What Some People Have Accomplished

Howard: Obtained a college degree and started 15 years ago in a show promotion/booking agency. He is now a tour production manager for a national entertainment act and earns more than $250,000 a year, with excellent benefits.

Mark: Was a college activities student, then a lighting technician, moved into theatre promotion, and is now making $60,000 a year working for a major promotion agency.

George: Left school in England at 15 and worked in various discos and nightclubs as a disc jockey. Took up an interest in lighting, went back to college, and studied electrical engineering. Moved to Rome and soon became head lighting director for a large concert touring company, working with U2, Peter Gabriel, Ray Charles, B.B. King, and many other stars. He is now vice president of marketing for one of New Jersey's leading lighting companies.

And, last but not least...

RICHARD E. TILLEY built his first light board out of a wooden wine box and household wall switches when he was in high school for a local garage band. In the twelve years since, he has provided lighting services for large corporations such as General Motors, Chubb Insurance, Prudential Base, Shearing Plough Pharmaceuticals, Six Flags Great Adventure, and the Bicentennial celebration at the North Terminal of the Statue of Liberty. Hundreds of entertainers and politicians have also used his professional talents. They include Stevie B, Expose, Sammy Davis, Jr., Ray Charles, Eddy Money, The Coasters, Jerry Lee Lewis, Hennie Youngman, Charlie Daniels, then-Vice President George Bush, N.J. Governor Thomas Kean, and Gary Hart. Universities such as Rutgers, Trenton, Kean, NYU, Drew, and Princeton have hired Rich to work on projects, one being the dance company that Brooke Shields was with at Princeton.

When Rich first entered the market, club shows were a major source of work, until stricter alcohol laws caused many of the clubs to close. While on the club circuit, he traveled extensively throughout the United States and overseas.

Rich is the president of Circuit Lighting Inc. in New Jersey, which designs, rents and sells lighting systems all over the world. His current emphasis is on small to mid-sized musical productions, corporate video lighting, and educational facility lighting systems.

14

Clothes *Do* Make
The Actor!

Rosemary Ponzo
Costume Designer

Costume Design is one of the most important—if sometimes least-heralded—facets of the entertainment business. As Audrey Hepburn put it at the 1986 Academy Awards:

> If clothes make the man, then certainly the costume designer makes the actor. The costume designer is not only essential, (but) is vital, for it is they who create the look of the character without which no performance can succeed. Theirs is a monumental job, for they must be not only artists but technicians, researchers, and historians. I am happy to honor these tireless, talented men and women who I have so much depended on.

The costume designer's main function is to "realize" the character in the play, TV or film via the clothing he or she wears.

The designer reads the script, then comes up with a concept and formulates it with a metaphor. This is in conjunction with the production designer (who designs the sets) and the director. Color schemes, fabrics, and trimmings all come into play at this time.

What Your Day Might Include

A typical day for a costume designer on the TV/film set will include:

- Looking over the schedule of the day's shoot
- Preparing wardrobe for each scene
- Checking the continuity
- Staying flexible—there may be changes!
- Enjoying the experience of working with other artists and technicians who are masters of their craft

If You'd Like To Dress Julia Roberts...

...or Mel Gibson, the starting point is as an assistant to the costume designer/stylist. In this position, you would be under the guidance of the costume designer—his or her right hand man/woman—making sure all of the costume pieces are in place for the various scenes of the TV or film. You would probably do the shopping for the "perfect" accessory and keep a record of all of the garments as they are shot for each show or scene.

Taking care of the actors is also a must. Knowing how to help them feel the most confident in their costume is a talent in itself. The assistant costume designer should have the same confidence in his or her work as the costume designer. If the costume designer is absent, the assistant must be able to take his or her place without anyone necessarily noticing a dropoff in skill.

To ensure continuity, as each scene in costume is shot, the assistant will take a Polaroid photograph of the costume and list the clothing and accessories. In case the scene needs to be re-shot, there will be a record of it from which the assistant can prepare that costume for the re-shoot.

Education

College is necessary—you may even want to obtain an M.F.A. in Costume/Theatre Design. A costume designer must be able to sketch and render costume drawings, plus have a thorough knowledge of fabrications and draping ability. Knowledge of costume and theatre history is also a must. There is also a union just for costume designers and stylists—the Costume Designers Guild. Entry is by examination or professional presentation of your portfolio and work experience.

Is Designing For You?

An ideal candidate for any entry-level position in this field is a person who really considers costume design as a life's work. As a great artist, it should be handled in the same manner—striving and doing whatever is necessary to continue creating. A strongly motivated person is important. You must be able to be flexible working with all the various characters of theatre, TV, and film. Stick to it, and never give up the attitude that you can become the best costume designer.

The goal which I personally have kept in mind is to achieve the highest goal or award: The Academy Award for Best Costume Design in Film. The Emmy for Best Costume Design in Television.

Splurge on with passion for your work.

A native of New York, **ROSEMARY PONZO** began her career with the motion picture "Sudden Death. Other film credits include: "White Hot," starring Danny Aiello, "Real Cowboy," "Once Again," and "Crossing The Bridge," to name a few.

She has designed over 22 television commercials, music videos for MTV, and the theatrical presentation of "A Bouquet for Mr Zeigfield," "A Comedy of No Manners," "Lulu-Pandora's Box," and an array of every Cole Porter musical under the sun.

Rosemary is a current member of the United Scenic Artist and Costume Designers Guild in Hollywood. She holds a M.F.A. from the Fashion Institute and has attended NYU's graduate school for film.

15

Internships: Getting Them And Making Them Work For You

**Helena Mitchell Greene, Ph. D., Director—
Office Of Television & Radio, Rutgers University**

Lights, camera, action! Working in television and radio is all of these.

And none of these.

As you can well imagine, positions at television and radio facilities are very diverse. They range from jobs in the administrative offices to jobs where all you do is studio/field/location shooting. From glamour and excitement to sheer hard work and perhaps even drudgery.

When you apply for that internship, choose your target stations according to what you want to learn...not just because you can get an internship there or it's close to home!

According to *Broadcast Magazine*, there are more than 10,800 radio stations, almost 1,500 television stations, and more than 10,800 cable systems in operation. If you add universities and colleges, corporations, community organizations, and other media-savvy outfits with television and radio production facilities, you are looking at probably *more than 25,000 opportunities for an internship*. And that's just domestically—internationally, there are even more opportunities.

Start Right Where You Are

If you have not yet taken a communications course, sign up for one that will give you a well-rounded view of the industry. By your junior or senior year, you can target a particular area of communications—research, management, operations, writing, or acting. A liberal arts or international specialty is also valued by many in the field.

Start With Who You Know

There are several great resources available on college campuses to get you going. Some sources include: instructors with contacts at local television and radio stations or cable franchises; placement offices who list internships; and, if you go to a larger college or university, your campus radio/television station or production facility.

A good source of leads for internships at major U.S. and Canadian radio and television stations is *Internships, Vol. 5: Radio & Television, Broadcasting & Production* (Career Press, 1991), the companion volume to this book, which lists thousands of internships at hundreds of stations.

If you are hoping to land a summer internship in your own town (and, therefore, need listings of every station out there), consult *Broadcasting Yearbook* (see Appendix B), which lists television and radio stations by state and city. You can find this book at your local or school library.

And no matter where you want to intern, in radio or television, at a large or small station, talk to as many people as you can about every aspect of the industry.

Start Reading

Let's assume you have had a communications course or two. What do you really know, and what do you really want to know? Do you want to know how a radio or television program is produced, or how the show is created, developed, funded and distributed? Are you interested in general station operations, engineering, research, community services, or administration? Or do you just want to work on the *Oprah Winfrey Show?*

If you have a textbook that details positions at television or radio stations, dust it off and peruse it again—if not, check one out of the library (and, obviously, read the rest of the articles in this *Career Directory!*). Read up on the facts of various television and radio stations. There are several fact books in most libraries that will give you the vital statistics on a station: how large it is, who the staff directors are, how many hours they broadcast, the type of license it holds (commercial or educational), station formats for radio, target audiences, and much more.

(Note: A production facility like Rutgers may have to be approached directly since it is not a broadcasting outlet and therefore does not appear in the industry fact books. Ask for the literature of production facilities as well since some, like Rutgers, are producers of programming for the Public Broadcasting Service and provide valuable experience.)

Start Preparing But Don't Panic

You are about to experience what the real world is like. Get ready mentally.

If you really like classical music and the only internship opening is at a hard rock radio station, think twice. Have you explored all your options? Did you consider the campus station or area businesses that prepare radio spots? Or were you just looking at ABC, NBC, and CBS? Perhaps now is also the time to go back and revisit places that rejected you. On more than one occasion, a student drops an internship and a position reopens. Don't let ten rejections panic you. After all, you only need one job—make it the right one.

Make a list of what you *must* get out of your internship experience, what you would optimally *like* to get out of it, and where you are willing to compromise. Having made this list, hope for the best. What unfolds in the day-to-day workplace of an internship may be the best or worst experience you have ever had. Just like a real job.

Getting Started

You arrive at your chosen internship, and, professionally attired, you begin. But what do you begin *doing?* The larger the television or radio facility, the more specialized your assignments will probably be; the smaller the station, the more diverse the duties.

On your first day, try to meet with your supervisor. Discuss the internship description and share information on yourself that will help him or her prioritize your assignments. Also ask about the basic operations of the facility.

It's important to establish some initial rapport with those around you—it will come in handy later and make your internship more interesting and less stressful right away. Learn the techniques of interpersonal communications. If you have a shy personality, practice asking questions. If you tend to be abrasive, practice asking questions more diplomatically.

Communication skills become very important when, three weeks into the internship, you are still xeroxing and haven't gained any useful experience. Try not to wait *that* long, but if you have, now is the time to talk with your supervisor again. Explain how much you looked forward to this internship, how you chose that station because of its fine reputation, how excited you are by all the activity around you, and how you would like to be a bigger part of it. Let them know that although you realize xeroxing is important, your school/mother/father/teacher is holding you responsible for the internship job description you signed on for.

Xeroxing And...

Finally, try to reach some kind of compromise. Let your supervisor know you want to help and learn at the same time. You value this opportunity, and you have a lot of natural attributes that could be useful around the station. For example, you have good people skills, reading skills, research skills, whatever. You have a good eye, a good ear, a strong back. If you have previous work experience or other background that's important, use that information also. Let them know you've worked in a bookstore (research, math, people skills), you had an out-of-the-mainstream job (diversity), you paint or like photography (creativity/camera skills), or you have a good voice (radio).

At this point, both you and your supervisor will hopefully have decided to expand your duties beyond xeroxing, and life should be looking up again. If it seems appropriate, suggest a rotation into another station area you have really taken an interest in. After all, with all that xeroxing you've been doing, I hope you've at least been *glancing* at what you've been copying!

Working At It

Internships are jobs. The experience you get in some internships will actually be at a higher level than when you first enter the workforce. At others, the experience may be inadequate for much of anything except as an entry on your resume. Turn your internship into the best experience you can. As soon as you have finished an assignment, volunteer to take on another. Don't lay back.

Some students think because they only do "what no one else wants to," that no one else is looking. Wrong. You are *always* being observed. (And should act as if you are even if you *aren't!*) The gossip mill is not just for full-time employees—it extends to that "young kid," as well. If the word goes out that "the kid is sharp," you will soon see additional assignments coming your way. If the word gets out that "the kid is sloppy, slow and inattentive," you will be doomed to the xerox machine.

Be helpful. Be cheerful. Be optimistic. Just like any worker, there will be many days you fake it. But, hey, you're in television! *Act* like it. You're in radio! *Sound* like it.

Keeping Your Internship In Perspective

Lights, camera, action! Did it happen for you?

The key to understanding the role of internships is to recognize that the experience is one of the most valuable lessons you will ever learn. Either you will decide to make a career in television or radio, or you will toss it aside as a career option. You win in either case because you found out early enough what you want to spend the rest of your life doing...or *not* doing.

You have also learned some techniques for making it in the real world—both good and bad. You had a chance to "play work" and observe, not just read about it in a text. You made contacts and had a chance to network. You have an entry on your resume that shows you have experience "out in the industry." If you were interning purely for school credit, you got some. If you were getting paid, you've earned money for other personal goals.

Letting Your Internship Work For You

Your graduation is down the road. From the time of your internship until the time you graduate, plan an approach to maximize the more than 25,000 "options" available to you. And remember that, as large as that number seems, it is increasing all the time: Each year there are many new business startups, plus stations with construction permits (1,725), so increase the 25,000 by another 2,500. Of course, there are failures, mergers, and layoffs. Still, the future is bright—telecommunications is one of the fastest growing segments in our economy.

How important is that internship? Most employers in the telecommunications industry *expect* an internship in your background. They want the employee to have both a post secondary degree *and* some experience. And an internship counts.

Stay Flexible

Once you graduate, the search starts all over again—but now you're looking for a job, which may be even harder to get than that internship you spent months pursuing! Should you move to find that entry-level job? In the majority of cases, you will *have* to relocate to find a job in the industry. With so many "seasoned" broadcast personnel being laid off and looking for jobs, the competition can be quite fierce. At the networks and network affiliates in the top markets, don't expect to just move to the area and land a job in weeks...or even months.

Your best bet is to use those contacts you've made, talk to lots of people at the places you want to go (not just in the personnel department), and keep up the search. Sometimes luck comes into play (it did for me), but it still pays to have this advice in the back of your mind.

Your first job will probably *not* be your first choice. If the job is of your choice, it will probably be in a small market. It may not be at a television or radio station. That's okay. Today there are a tremendous number of media-conscious outfits, so don't despair. These smaller operations often give the best practical experience—you get to do it all. At a larger television, radio or media outfit, it will take longer to move into the position you really want, because they have a larger pool of experienced personnel to choose from.

Keep Your Chin Up

Having hired interns and worked with them for more than two decades, those who were successful shared two important attributes—attitude and communication. Work on developing a positive attitude. See problems as projects, see disappointments as awakenings, see negativity as energy that can be turned around. You want to work in communications, so learn to communicate. Explain what you really mean, be diplomatic yet honest, keep dialogue flowing even when it seems impossible.

Is working in television and radio really worth it? You've had a taste of it, what do you think? It's rough, it's easy, there are long days, and days of just sitting around. It can be exciting, dynamic, and constantly changing. It's seeing a project you've worked on completed and delivered to millions of viewers or listeners to make them laugh or cry or think.

Is This Industry For You?

Only you can decide the worth of turning your internship into a long-term career. Synthesize all you've learned and all you think you *can* learn in the years ahead. Statistics say the average person will have four career changes in their lifetime. This can be your first.

It can also be one of the other three.

If you decide to stay the course, work at it. Think of it the way many of us in the industry do to help weather the stormy times—the television and radio business is truly the greatest show on earth!

HELENA MITCHELL GREENE has a background that spans a wide range of pursuits, from innovative programs in broadcasting and government policy management to college administrator and faculty member. Helena's current position combines her interests in broadcasting, education and policy. The office serves the university's instructional and public service commitment through television, radio, advanced technologies, and statewide planning networks. At the same time, it produces television and radio programming for the Public Broadcasting Service (PBS).

Before Rutgers, Helena spent several years in Canada and the Caribbean managing communcations operations. Prior to working abroad, she was the director of telecommunications development for the U.S. Department of Commerce National Telecommunications and Information Administration. Originally a New Yorker, she has served in management at WNET/13 and WNYC-TV/AM-FM, where she was responsible for producing broadcast programming.

Dr. Greene received her Ph.D. and Master's from Syracuse University and her Bachelor's from SUNY at Brockport. She has been in the industry since 1970, and has always involved students as interns in her programs. She has been an editor, author and writer on numerous communications, policy and ethnic publications.

Section 2

The
Job Search
Process

16

Getting Started: Self Evaluation And Career Objectives

Getting a job may be a relatively simple one-step or couple-of weeks-process or a complex, months-long operation.

Starting, nurturing and developing a career (or even a series of careers) is a lifelong process.

What we'll be talking about in the five chapters that together form our Job Search Process are those basic steps to take, assumptions to make, things to think about if you want a job—especially a first job in radio or television broadcasting or production. But when these steps—this process—are applied and expanded over a lifetime, most if not all of them are the same procedures, carried out over and over again, that are necessary to develop a successful, lifelong, professional career.

What does all this have to do with putting together a resume and portfolio, writing a cover letter, heading off for interviews, and the other "traditional" steps necessary to get a job? Whether your college graduation is just around the corner or a far-distant memory, you will continuously need to focus, evaluate and re-evaluate your response to the ever-changing challenge of your future: Just what do you want to do with the rest of your life? Whether you like it or not, you're all looking for that "entry-level opportunity."

You're already one or two steps ahead of the competition—you're sure (pretty sure?) you want to pursue a career in some area of radio or television. By heeding the advice of the many professionals who have written chapters for this *Career Directory*—and utilizing the extensive entry-level job, organization and publication listings we've included—you're well on your way to fulfilling that dream. But there are some key decisions and time-consuming preparations to make if you want to transform that hopeful dream into a real, live job.

The actual process of finding the right station, right career path, and, most importantly, the right first job, begins long before you start mailing out resumes to potential employers. The choices and decisions you make now are not irrevocable, but this first job will have a definite impact on the career options you leave yourself. To help you make some of the right decisions and choices along the way (and avoid the most notable traps and pitfalls), the following chapters will lead you through a series of organized steps. If the entire job search process we are recommending here is properly executed, it will undoubtedly help you land exactly the job you want.

If you're currently in high school and hope, after college, to land a job at a radio or TV station, then attending the right college, choosing the right major, and getting the summer work experience many stations look for are all important steps. Read the section of this *Career Directory* that covers the particular job specialty in which you're interested—many of the contributors have recommended colleges or graduate programs they favor.

If you're hoping to jump right into any of these jobs with*out* a college degree or other professional training, our best and only advice is—don't do it. As you'll soon see in the detailed information included in the *Job Opportunities Databank*, there are not *that* many job openings for students without a college degree. Those that do exist are generally clerical and will only rarely lead to promising careers.

The Concept Of A Job Search *Process*

These are the key steps in the detailed job search process we will cover in this and the following four chapters:

1. *Evaluating yourself*: Know thyself. What skills and abilities can you offer a prospective employer? What do you enjoy doing? What are your strengths and weaknesses? What do you *want* to do?

2. *Establishing your career objectives*: Where do you want to be next year, three years, five years from now? What do you ultimately want to accomplish in your career and your life?

3. *Creating a station target list*: How to prepare a "Hit List" of potential employers—researching them, matching their needs with your skills, and starting your job search assault. Preparing station information sheets and evaluating your chances.

4. *Networking for success:* Learning how to utilize every contact, every friend, every relative, and anyone else you can think of to break down the barriers facing any would-be professional. How to organize your home office to keep track of your communications and stay on top of your job campaign.

5. *Preparing your resume:* How to encapsulate years of school and little actual work experience into a professional, selling resume. Learning when and how to use it.

6. *Preparing cover letters:* The many ordinary and the all-too-few extraordinary cover letters, the kind that land interviews and jobs.

7. *Interviewing:* How to make the interview process work for you—from the first "hello" to the first day on the job.

We won't try to kid you—it *is* a lot of work. To do it right, you have to get started early, probably quite a bit earlier than you'd planned. Frankly, we recommend beginning this process one full year prior to the day you plan to start work.

So if you're in college, the end of your junior year is the right time to begin your research and preparations. That should give you enough time during summer vacation to set up your files and begin your library research.

Whether you're in college or graduate school, one item may need to be planned even earlier—allowing enough free time in your schedule of classes for interview preparations and appointments. Waiting until your senior year to "make some time" is already too late. Searching for a full-time job is itself a full-time job! Though you're naturally restricted by your schedule, it's not difficult to plan ahead and prepare for your upcoming job search. Try to leave at least a couple of free mornings or afternoons a week. A day or even two without classes is even better.

Otherwise, you'll find yourself, crazed and distracted, trying to prepare for an interview in the ten-minute period between your "Media in the '90s" lecture and your Broadcasting 201 seminar. Not the best way to make a first impression and certainly not the way you want to approach an important meeting.

The Self-Evaluation Process

Learning about who you are, what you want to be, what you *can* be, are critical first steps in the job search process and, unfortunately, the ones most often ignored by job seekers everywhere, especially students eager to leave the ivy behind and plunge into the "real world." But avoiding this crucial self evaluation can hinder your progress and even damage some decent prospects.

Why? Because in order to land a job with a station at which you'll actually be happy, you need to be able to identify those stations and/or job descriptions that best match your own skills, likes and strengths. The more you know about yourself, the more you'll bring to this process and the more accurate the "match-ups." You'll be able to structure your presentation (resume, cover letter, interviews) to stress your most marketable skills and talents (and, dare we say it, conveniently avoid your weaknesses?). Later, you'll be able to evaluate potential employers and job offers on the basis of your own needs and desires. This spells the difference between waking up in the morning ready to enthusiastically tackle a new day of challenges and shutting off the alarm in the hopes the day (and your job) will just disappear.

Creating Your Self-Evaluation Form

Take a sheet of lined notebook paper. Set up eight columns across the top—Strengths, Weaknesses, Skills, Hobbies, Courses, Experience, Likes, Dislikes.

Now, fill in each of these columns according to these guidelines:

Strengths: Describe personality traits you consider your strengths (and try to look at them as an employer would)—e.g., persistence, organization, ambition, intelligence, logic, assertiveness, aggression, leadership, etc.

Weaknesses: The traits you consider glaring weaknesses—e.g., impatience, conceit, etc. (And remember: Look at these as a potential employer would. Don't assume that the personal traits you consider weaknesses will necessarily be considered negatives in the business world. You may be "easily bored," a trait that led to lousy grades early on because teachers couldn't keep you interested in the subjects they were teaching. Well, many entrepreneurs need ever-changing challenges. Strength or weakness?)

Skills: Any skill you have, whether you think it's marketable or not. Everything from basic business skills—like typing, word processing and stenography—to computer, accounting or teaching experience and foreign language literacy. Don't forget possibly obscure but marketable skills like "good telephone voice."

Hobbies: The things you enjoy doing that, more than likely, have no overt connection to career objectives. These should be distinct from the skills listed above, and may include activities such as reading, games, travel, sports and the like. While these may not be marketable in any general sense, they may well be useful in specific circumstances. (If you love sports and have interned at a couple of radio or TV stations over summers, you may be perfect for that entry-level job as support staff for the Sports Desk. And your "hobbies"—and the knowledge and expertise they've given you—may just get it for you!)

Courses: All the general subject areas (history, literature, etc.) and/or specific courses you've taken which may be marketable, you really enjoyed, or both.

Experience: Just the specific functions you performed at any part-time (school year) or full-time (summer) jobs.

Likes: List all your "likes"—those important considerations that you haven't listed any-where else yet. These might include the types of people you like to be with, the kind of environ-ment you prefer (city, country, large places, small places, quiet, loud, fast-paced, slow-paced), and anything else which hasn't shown up somewhere on this form. However, try not to include entries which refer to specific jobs or stations. We'll list those on another form.

Dislikes: All the people, places and things you can easily live without.

Now assess the "marketability" of each item you've listed. In other words, are some of your likes, skills or courses easier to match to a specific job description, or do they have little to do with a specific job or station? Mark highly marketable skills with an "H." Use "M" to characterize those skills which may be marketable in a particular set of circumstances, "L" for those with minimal potential application to any job.

Referring back to the same list, decide if you'd enjoy using your marketable skills or talents as part of your everyday job—"Y" for yes, "N" for no. You may type 80 words a minute but truly despise typing or worry that stressing it too much will land you on the permanent clerical staff. If so, mark typing with an "N." (Keep one thing in mind—just because you dislike typing shouldn't mean you absolutely won't accept a job that requires it. Many do. And even if one doesn't, the continued computerization of all industries will virtually require everyone to type—if only enough to use a computer—within the decade.)

Now, go over the entire form carefully and look for inconsistencies.

The Value Of A Second Opinion

There is a familiar misconception about the self-evaluation process that gets in the way of many new job applicants—the belief that it is a process which must be accomplished in isolation. Nothing could be further from the truth. Just because the family doctor tells you you need an operation doesn't mean you run right off to the hospital. Prudence dictates that you check out the opinion with another physician. Getting such a "second opinion"—someone else's, not just your own—is a valuable practice throughout the job search process, as well.

So after you've completed the various exercises in this chapter, review them with a friend, relative or parent. These second opinions may reveal some aspects of your self description on which you and the rest of the world differ. If so, discuss them, learn from them, and, if necessary, change some conclusions. Should everyone concur with your self evaluation, you will be reassured that your choices are on target.

Establishing Your Career Objectives

For better or worse, you now know something more of who and what you are. But we've yet to establish and evaluate another important area—your overall needs, desires and goals. Where are you going? What do you want to accomplish?

If you're getting ready to graduate from college or graduate school, the next five years are the most critical period of your whole career. You need to make the initial transition from college to the workplace, establish yourself in a new and completely unfamiliar environment, and begin to build the professional credentials necessary to achieve your career goals.

If that strikes you as a pretty tall order, well, it *is*. It's tough to face, but face it you must: No matter what your college, major or degree, all you represent right now is potential. How you package that potential and what you eventually make of it is completely up to you. And it's an unfortunate fact that many companies will take a professional with barely a year or two experience over *any* newcomer, no matter how promising. Smaller stations, especially, can rarely afford to hire someone who can't begin contributing immediately.

So you have to be prepared to take your comparatively modest skills and experience and package them in a way that will get you interviewed and hired. Quite a challenge.

Is This Industry Right For *You?*

Presuming you now have a much better idea of yourself and where you'd like to be—job-, career- and life-wise in the foreseeable future—let's make sure some of your basic assumptions are right. We presume you purchased this *Career Directory* because you're considering a career in some area of the radio or television business. Are you sure? Do you know enough about the industry as a whole and the particular part you're heading for to decide whether it's right for you? Probably not. So start your research *now*—learn as much about your potential career as you now know about

In Appendix A, we've listed all the trade organizations associated with the radio and television businesses. Where possible, we've included details on educational information available from these associations, but you should certainly consider writing each of the pertinent ones, letting them know you're interested in a career in their area of specialization, and that you would appreciate whatever help and advice they're willing to impart. You'll find many sponsor seminars and conferences throughout the country, some of which you may be able to attend.

In Appendix B, we've listed the trade publications dedicated to the highly specific interests of the various areas of the radio/TV community. These magazines are generally not available at newsstands (unless you live in or near New York City), but you may be able to obtain back issues at your local library (most major libraries have extensive collections of such journals) or by writing to the magazines' circulation/subscription departments.

You may also try writing to the publishers and/or editors of these publications. State in your cover letter what area of the business you're considering and ask them for whatever help and advice they can offer. But be specific. These are busy professionals and they do not have the time or the inclination to simply "tell me everything you can about becoming a producer."

If you can afford it now, we strongly suggest subscribing to whichever trade magazines are applicable to the specialty you're considering. If you can't subscribe to all of them, make it a point to regularly read the copies that arrive at your local public or college library.

These publications may well provide the most imaginative and far-reaching information for your job search. Even a quick perusal of an issue or two will give you an excellent "feel" for the industry. After reading only a few articles, you'll already get a handle on what's happening in the field and some of the industry's peculiar and particular jargon. Later, more detailed study will aid you in your search for a specific job.

Authors of the articles themselves may well turn out to be important resources. If an article is directly related to your chosen specialty, why not call the author and ask some questions? You'd be amazed how willing many of these professionals will be to talk to you and answer your questions. They may even tell you about job openings at their stations! (But *do* use common sense—authors will not *always* respond graciously to your invitation to "chat about the business." And don't be *too* aggressive here.)

You'll find such research to be a double-edged sword. In addition to helping you get a handle on whether the area you've chosen is really right for you, you'll slowly learn enough about particular specialties, stations, programs, the industry, etc., to actually sound like you know what you're talking about when you hit the pavement looking for your first job. And nothing is better than sounding like a pro...except being one.

Radio/TV Is It. Now What?

After all this research, we're going to assume you've reached that final decision—you really *do* want a career in radio or television. It is with this vague certainty that all too many of you will race off, hunting for any station willing to give you a job. You'll manage to get interviews at a couple and, smiling brightly, tell everyone you meet, "I want a career in radio (or television)." The interviewers, unfortunately, will all ask the same awkward question—"What *exactly* do you want to do at our station?"—and that will be the end of that.

It is simply not enough to narrow your job search to a specific industry. And so far, that's all you've done. You must now establish a specific career objective—the job you want to start, the career you want to pursue. Just knowing that you "want to get into radio or TV" doesn't mean anything to anybody. If that's all you can tell an interviewer, it demonstrates a lack of research into the industry itself and your failure to think ahead.

Interviewers will *not* welcome you with open arms if you're still vague about your career goals. If you've managed to get an "informational interview" with an executive whose station currently has no job openings, what is he supposed to do with your resume after you leave? Who should he send it to for future consideration? Since *you* don't seem to know exactly what you want to do, how's *he* going to figure it out? Worse, he'll probably resent your asking him to function as your personal career counselor.

Remember, the more specific your career objective, the better your chances of finding a job. It's that simple and that important. Naturally, before you declare your objective to the world, check once again to make sure your specific job target matches the skills and interests you defined in your self evaluation. Eventually, you may want to state such an objective on your resume and "To obtain an entry-level position as a radio salesperson at a metropolitan station" is quite a bit better than "I want a career in broadcasting." Do not consider this step final until you can summarize your job/career objective in a single, short, accurate sentence.

17

Targeting Prospective Employers & Networking For Success

As you move along the job search path, one fact will quickly become crystal clear—it is primarily a process of **elimination**: Your task is to consider and research as many options as possible, then—for good reasons—*eliminate* as many as possible, attempting to continually narrow your focus.

The essential first step is to establish some criteria to evaluate potential employers. This will enable you to identify your target stations, those for whom you'd really like to work. (This process, as we've pointed out, is not specific to any industry or field; the same steps, with perhaps some research resource variations, are applicable to any job, any company, any industry.)

Take a sheet of blank paper and divide it into three vertical columns. Title it "Target Station —Ideal Profile." Call the left-hand column "Musts," the middle column "Preferences," and the right-hand column "Nevers."

We've listed a series of questions below. After considering each question, decide whether a particular criteria *must* be met, whether you would simply *prefer* it, or *never* would consider it at all. If there are other criteria you consider important, feel free to add them to the list below and mark them accordingly on your Profile.

1. What are your geographical preferences? U. S.? Canada? Europe? Anywhere you can get a job???

2. If you prefer to work in the U.S. or Canada, what area, state(s) or province(s)? If overseas, what area or countries?

3. Do you prefer a large city, small city, town, or somewhere as far away from civilization as possible?

4. In regard to question 3, any specific preferences?

5. Do you prefer a warm or cold climate?

6. Do you prefer a large or small station? Radio or television? Or production house? Or corporate department?

7. Do you mind relocating right now? Do you want to work for a station/company with a reputation for *frequently* relocating top people?

8. Do you mind travelling frequently? What percent do you consider reasonable? (Make sure this matches the normal requirements of the job specialization you're considering.)

9. What salary would you *like* to receive (put in the "Preference" column)? What's the *lowest* salary you'll accept (in the "Must" column)?

10. Are there any benefits (such as an expense account, medical and/or dental insurance, company car, etc.) you must or would like to have?

11. Are you planning to attend graduate school at some point in the future; if so, is a tuition reimbursement plan important to you?

12. Do you feel a formal training program necessary?

It's important to keep revising this new form, just as you should continue to update your Self-Evaluation Form. After all, it contains the criteria by which you will judge every potential employer. Armed with a complete list of such criteria, you're now ready to find all the stations that match them.

Targeting Individual Radio/TV Stations

To begin creating your initial list of targeted stations, start with the *Job Opportunities Databank*. We've listed more than 200 top radio and television networks and stations—including, for the first time, opportunities at stations across Canada. These companies completed questionnaires we supplied, providing us (and you!) with a plethora of data concerning their over-all operations, hiring practices, and other important information on entry-level job opportunities. This latter information includes key contacts (names), the average number of entry-level people they hire each year, along with complete job descriptions and requirements. All of the detailed information in these chapters was provided by the stations themselves. To our knowledge, it is available *only* in this *Career Directory.*

We have attempted to include information on the major networks and largest stations that represent most of the entry-level jobs out there. But there are, of course, many other stations of all sizes and shapes that you may also wish to research. In the next section, we will discuss some other reference books you can use to obtain more information on the stations we've listed, as well as those we haven't.

Other Reference Tools

In order to obtain some of the detailed information you need, you will probably need to do further research, either in the library or by meeting and chatting with people familiar with the stations in which you're interested.

For general research—pertinent to all companies—you might want to start with How To Find Information About Companies (Washington Researchers); the Encyclopedia of Business Information Sources (Gale Research, Book Tower, Detroit, MI 48226); and/or the Guide to American Directories (B. Klein Publications, P.O. Box 8503, Coral Springs, FL 33065), which lists directories for over 3,000 fields.

If you want to work for one of the associations which serves the broadcasting industry, we've listed all those in Appendix A. Other associations may be researched in the Encyclopedia of Associations (Gale Research Co.) or National Trade and Professional Associations of the United States (Columbia Books, Inc., 777 14th St., NW, Suite 236, Washington, DC 20005).

There are, in addition, many general corporate directories, biographical indexes, statistical abstracts, etc., etc.—from Gale Research, Dun & Bradstreet, Standard & Poor's, Ward's and others— which may give you additional information on major networks, stations, ancillary companies and their executives. These volumes—and more such directories seem to be published every month— should all be available in the reference (and/or business) section of your local library.

The most important directories specific to the broadcasting industry—along with all pertinent trade publications—are listed in Appendix B.

One last note on potential sources of leads: The Oxbridge Directory of Newsletters, 7th Edition (available from Oxbridge Communications, 150 Fifth Ave., Suite 301, New York, NY 10011) lists details of more than 17,000 newsletters in a plethora of industries and might well give you some ideas and names.

And the Professional Exhibits Directory (Gale Research Co.) lists more than 2,000 trade shows and conventions. Such shows are excellent places to "run into" radio and TV pros and offer unexpected opportunities to learn about the industry "from the horse's mouth."

Ask The Person Who Owns One

Some years ago, this advice was used as the theme for a highly successful automobile advertising campaign. The prospective car buyer was encouraged to find out about the product by asking the (supposedly) most trustworthy judge of all—someone who was already an owner.

You can use the same approach in your job search. You all have relatives or friends already out in the workplace—these are your best sources of information about those industries. Cast your net in as wide a circle as possible. Contact these valuable resources. You'll be amazed at how readily they will answer your questions. I suggest you check the criteria list at the beginning of this chapter to formulate your own list of pertinent questions. Ideally and minimally you will want to learn: how the industry is doing, what its long-term prospects are, the kinds of personalities they favor (aggressive, low key), rate of employee turnover, and the availability of training.

Making Friends And Influencing People

Networking is a term you have probably heard; it is definitely a key aspect of any successful job search and a process you must master.

Informational interviews and **job interviews** are the two primary outgrowths of successful networking.

Referrals, an aspect of the networking process, entail using someone else's name, credentials and recommendation to set up a receptive environment when seeking a job interview.

All of these terms have one thing in common: Each depends on the actions of other people to put them in motion.

So what *is* networking? *How* do you build your own network? And *why* do you need one in the first place? The balance of this chapter answers all of those questions and more.

Get your telephone ready. It's time to make some friends.

Not The World's Oldest Profession, But...

As Gekko, the high-rolling corporate raider, sneers in the movie *Wall Street:* "Any schmuck can analyze stock charts. What separates the players from the sheep is **information.**" Networking is the process of creating your own group of relatives, friends and acquaintances who can feed you the information *you* need to find a job—identifying where the jobs are and giving you the personal introductions and background data necessary to pursue them.

If the job market were so well-organized that details on all employment opportunities were immediately available to all applicants, there would be no need for such a process. Rest assured the job market is *not* such a smooth-running machine—most applicants are left very much to their own devices. Build and use your own network wisely and you'll be amazed at the amount of useful job intelligence you will turn up.

While the term networking didn't gain prominence until the 1970s, it is by no means a new phenomenon. A selection process that connects people of similar skills, backgrounds and/or attitudes—in other words, networking—has been in existence in a variety of forms for centuries. Attend any Ivy League school and you're automatically part of its very special centuries-old network.

Major law firms are known to favor candidates from a preferred list of law schools—the same ones the senior partners attended. Washington, D.C. and Corporate America have their own network—the same corporate bigwigs move back and forth from boardroom to Cabinet Room.

The Academia-Washington connection is just as strong—notice the number of Harvard professors (e.g., Henry Kissinger, John Kenneth Galbraith) who call Washington their second home? No matter which party is in power, certain names just keep surfacing as Secretary of This or Undersecretary of That. No, networking is not new. It's just left its ivory tower and become a well-publicized process *anyone* can and should utilize in their lifelong career development.

And it works.

Remember your own reaction when you were asked to recommend someone for a job, club or school office? You certainly didn't want to look foolish, so you gave it some thought and tried to recommend the best-qualified person that you thought would "fit in" with the rest of the group. It's a built-in screening process—what's more natural than recommending someone who's "our kind of _____?"

Creating The Ideal Network

As in most endeavors, there's a wrong way and a right way to network. The following tips will help you construct your own wide-ranging, information-gathering, interview-generating group—*your* network.

Diversify

Unlike the Harvard or Princeton network—confined to former graduates of each school—*your* network should be as diversified and wide-ranging as possible. You never know who might be in a position to help, so don't limit your group of friends. The more diverse they are, the greater the variety of information they may supply you with.

Don't Forget...

...to include everyone you know in your initial networking list: friends, relatives, social acquaintances, classmates, college alumni, professors, teachers; your dentist, doctor, family lawyer, insurance agent, banker, travel agent; elected officials in your community; ministers; fellow church members; local tradesmen; local business or social club officers. And everybody *they* know!

Be Specific

Make a list of the kinds of assistance you will require from those in your network, then make specific requests of each. Do they know of jobs at their facility? Can they introduce you to the proper executives? Have they heard something about or know someone at the hospital you're planning to interview with next week?

The more organized you are, the easier it will be to target the information you need and figure out who might have it. Calling everyone and simply asking for "whatever help you can give me" is unfair to the people you're calling and a less effective way to garner information you need.

Learn The Difference...

...between an **informational** interview and a **job** interview. The former requires you to cast yourself in the role of information gatherer; *you* are the interviewer and knowledge is your goal—about an industry, company, job function, key executive, etc. Such a meeting with someone already doing what you soon *hope* to be doing is by far the best way to find out everything you need to know...before you walk through the door and sit down for a formal job interview, at which time your purpose is more sharply defined: to get the job you're interviewing for.

If you learn of a specific job opening during an informational interview, you are in a position to find out details about the job, identify the interviewer and, possibly, even learn some things about him or her. In addition, presuming you get your contact's permission, you may be able to use his or her name as a referral.

(Be careful about referring to a specific job opening, even if your contact told you about it. It may not be something you're supposed to know about. By presenting your query as an open-ended question, you give your prospective employer the option of exploring your background without further commitment. If there is a job for which you're qualified, you'll find out soon enough.)

Value Your Contacts

Not everyone you call on your highly-diversified networking list will know about a job opening. It would be surprising if each one did. But what about *their* friends and colleagues? It's amazing how everyone knows someone who knows someone. Ask—you'll find that someone.

If someone has provided you with helpful information or an introduction to a friend or colleague, keep him or her informed about how it all turns out. A referral that's panned out should be reported to the person who opened the door for you in the first place. Such courtesy will be appreciated...and may lead to more contacts. If someone has nothing to offer today, a call back in the future is still appropriate and may pay off.

The lesson is clear: Keep your options open, your contact list alive. Detailed records of your network—whom you spoke with, when, what transpired, etc.—will help you keep track of your overall progress and organize what can be a complicated and involved process.

Keeping Track of The Interview Trail

Let's talk about record keeping again. If your networking works the way it's supposed to, you will be able to arrange a number of interviews. Experts have estimated that the average person could develop a contact list of 250 people. Even if we limit your initial list to only 100, if each of them gave you one referral, your list would suddenly have 200 names. Presuming that it will not be necessary or helpful to see all of them, it's certainly possible that such a list could lead to 100 informational and/or job interviews! Unless you keep accurate records, by the time you're on No. 50, you won't even remember the first dozen!

So get the results of each interview down on paper. Use whatever format with which you are comfortable. You should create some kind of file, folder or note card that is an "Interview Recap Record." It should be set up and contain something like the following:

Name: WII-AM
Address: 333 Broad St., NY, NY 10000
Phone: (212) 666-6666
Contact: Robert L. Jones
Type of Business: AM radio station—news format
Referral Contact: Mr. Fredericks, Fidelity National Bank
Date: June 23, 1991

At this point, you should add a one- or two-paragraph summary of what you found out at the meeting. Since these comments are for your eyes only, you should be both objective and subjective. State the facts—what you found out in response to your specific questions—but include your impressions—your estimate of the opportunities for further discussions, your chances for future consideration for employment.

There Are Rules, Just Like Any Game

It should already be obvious that the networking process is not only effective, but also quite deliberate in its objectives. There are two specific groups of people you must attempt to target: those who can give you information about an industry or career area and those who are potential employers. The line between these groups may often blur. Don't be concerned—you'll soon learn when (and how) to shift the focus from interview*er* to interview*ee*.

To simplify this process, follow a single rule: Show interest in the field or job area under discussion, but wait to be asked about actually working for that hospital. During your informational interviews, you will be surprised at the number of times the person you're interviewing turns to you and asks, "Would you be interested in…?" Consider carefully what's being asked and, if you *would* be interested in the position under discussion, make your feelings known.

What's It All About (Alfie)?

- To unearth current information about the industry, station and pertinent job functions. Remember: Your knowledge and understanding of broad industry trends, financial health, hiring opportunities, and the competitive picture are key.

- To investigate each station's hiring policies—who makes the decisions, who the key players are (personnel, staff managers), whether there's a hiring season, if they prefer applicants going direct or through recruiters, etc.

- To sell yourself—discuss your interests and research activities—and leave your calling card, your resume.

- To seek out advice on refining your job search process.

- To obtain the names of other persons (referrals) who can give you additional information on where the jobs are and what the market conditions are like.

- To develop a list of follow-up activities that will keep you visible to key contacts.

If The Process Scares You

Some of you will undoutedly be hesitant about, even fear, the networking process. It is not an unusual response—it is very human to want to accomplish things "on your own," without anyone's help. Understandable and commendable as such independence might seem, it is, in reality, an impediment if it limits your involvement in this important process. Networking has such universal application because *there is no other effective way to bridge the gap between job applicant and job.* Employers are grateful for its existence. You should be, too.

Whether you are a first-time applicant or reentering the work force now that the children are grown, the networking process will more than likely be your point of entry. Sending out mass mailings of your resume and answering the help wanted ads may well be less personal (and, therefore, "easier") approaches, but they will also be far less effective. The natural selection process of the networking phenomenon is your assurance that water does indeed seek its own level—you will be matched up with companies and job opportunities in which there is a mutual fit.

Six Good Reasons To Network

Many people fear the networking process because they think they are "bothering" others with their own selfish demands. Nonsense! There are good reasons—six of them, at least—why the people on your networking list will be *happy* to help you:

1) *Some day you will get to return the favor.* An ace insurance salesman built a successful business by offering low-cost coverage to first-year medical students. Ten years later, these now-successful practitioners remembered the company (and person) that helped them when they were just getting started. He gets new referrals every day.

2) *They, too, are seeking information.* Don't be surprised if you are asked questions that seem to have little or nothing to do with an actual job. The interviewer may well be trying to "keep his or her hand" on the pulse of current education in his or her field. Why not let the interviewer "audit" your course? It may be the reason he or she agreed to see you in the first place.

3) *Internal politics*—Some people will see you simply to make themselves appear powerful, implying to others in their organization that they have the authority to hire (they may or may not), an envied prerogative.

4) *They're "saving for a rainy day"*—Executives know that it never hurts to look and that maintaining a backlog of qualified candidates is a big asset when the floodgates open and supervisors are forced to hire quickly.

5) *They're just plain nice*—Some people will see you simply because they feel it's the decent thing to do or because they just can't say "no."

6) *They are looking themselves*—Some people will see you because they are anxious to do a friend (whoever referred you) a favor. Or because they have another friend seeking new talent, in which case you represent a referral *they* can make (part of their own continuing network process). You see, networking never *does* stop—it helps them and it helps you.

Before you proceed to the next chapter, begin making your contact list. You may wish to keep a separate sheet of paper or note card on each person (especially the dozen or so you think are most important), even a separate telephone list to make your communications easier and more efficient. However you set up your list, be sure to keep it up to date.

It won't be long before you'll be calling each and every name on the list.

18

Preparing Your Resume

Your resume is a one- or two-page summary of you—your education, skills, employment experience, and career objective(s). It is *not* a biography—just a quick way to identify and describe you to potential employers. Most importantly, its *real* purpose is to *sell* you to the radio or television station you want to work for. It must set you apart from all the other applicants (those competitors) out there.

So, as you sit down to formulate your resume, remember you're trying to present the pertinent information in a format and manner that will convince an executive to grant you an interview, the prelude to any job offer. (If you feel you need more help in resume preparation, or even in the entire job search area, we recommend Your First Resume by Ronald W. Fry.)

An Overview Of Resume Preparation

- **Know what you're doing**—your resume is a personal billboard of accomplishments. It must communicate your specific worth to a prospective employer.

- **Your language should be action-oriented,** full of "doing"-type words. And less is better than more. Be concise and direct; don't worry about complete sentences.

- **Be persuasive.** In those sections that allow you the freedom to do so, don't hesitate to communicate your worth in the strongest language. This does *not* mean a long list of self-congratulatory superlatives; it *does* mean truthful claims about your abilities and the evidence (educational, experiential) that supports them.

- **Don't be cheap or gaudy.** Don't hesitate to spend the few extra dollars necessary to present a professional-looking resume. Do avoid outlandish (and generally ineffective) gimmicks like over-sized or brightly-colored paper.

- **Find an editor.** Every good writer needs one, and you are *writing* your resume. At the very least, it will offer you a second set of eyes proofreading for embarrassing typos. But if you are fortunate enough to have a professional in the field—a recruiter or personnel executive—critique a draft, grab the opportunity.

- **If you're the next Michaelangelo,** so multi-talented that you can easily qualify for jobs in different career areas, don't hesitate to prepare two or more completely different resumes. This will enable you to change the emphasis on your education and skills according to the specific career objective on each resume, a necessary alteration that will correctly target each one.

- **Choose the proper format.** There are only three we recommend—chronological, functional and combination. It's important you use the one that's right for you.

The Records You Need

The resume-writing process begins with the assembly and organization of all the personal, educational and employment data from which you will choose the pieces that actually end up on paper. If this information is properly organized, writing your resume will be a relatively easy task, a simple process of just shifting data from one format (record-keeping sheets) to another (the resume format you'll use later in this chapter, including a fill-in-the-blanks form).

As you will soon see, there is a lot of information you'll need to keep track of. In order to avoid a fevered search for important information, take the time right now to designate a single location in which to store all your records. Our recommendation is either a filing cabinet or an expandable pocket portfolio. The latter is less expensive, yet it will still enable you to sort your records into an unlimited number of more-manageable categories.

Losing important report cards, citations, letters, etc., is easy to do if your life's history is scattered throughout your room or, even worse, your house! While copies of many of these items may be obtainable, why put yourself through all that extra work? Making good organization a habit will ensure that all the records you need to prepare your resume will be right where you need them *when* you need them.

For each of the categories summarized below, designate a separate file drawer or, at the very least, file folder in which pertinent records can be kept. Your own notes are important, but keeping actual report cards, award citations, letters, etc. is even more so. Here's what your record-keeping system should include:

Transcripts (Including GPA And Class Rank Information)

Transcripts are your school's official record of your academic history, usually available, on request, from your high school's guidance office or college registrar's office.

Your college may charge you for copies and "on request" doesn't mean "whenever you want"—you may have to wait some time for your request to be processed (so *don't* wait until the last minute!).

Your school-calculated GPA (Grade Point Average) is on the transcript. Most schools calculate this by multiplying the credit hours assigned to each course times a numerical grade equivalent (e.g., "A" = 4.0, "B" = 3.0, etc.), then dividing by total credits/courses taken. Class rank is simply a listing of GPAs, from highest to lowest.

Employment Records

Details on every part-time or full-time job you've held, including:

- Each employer's name, address and telephone number
- Name of supervisor

- Exact dates worked
- Approximate numbers of hours per week
- Specific duties and responsibilities
- Specific skills utilized
- Accomplishments, honors
- Copies of awards, letters of recommendation

Volunteer Activities

Just because you weren't paid for a specific job—stuffing envelopes for the local Republican candidate, being a Candy Striper, manning a drug hotline—doesn't mean that it wasn't significant or that you shouldn't include it on your resume. So keep the same detailed notes on these volunteer activities as you have on the jobs you've held:

- Each organization's name, address and telephone number
- Name of supervisor
- Exact dates worked
- Approximate numbers of hours per week
- Specific duties and responsibilities
- Specific skills utilized
- Accomplishments, honors
- Copies of awards, letters of recommendation

Extracurricular Activities

List all sports, clubs or other activities in which you've participated, either inside or outside school. For each, you should include:

- Name of activity/club/group
- Office(s) held
- Purpose of club/activity
- Specific duties/responsibilities
- Achievements, accomplishments, awards

Honors And Awards

Even if some of these honors are previously listed, the following specific data on every honor or award you receive should be kept in your awards folder:

- Award name
- Date and from whom received
- What it was for
- Any pertinent details

Military Records

Complete military history, if pertinent, including:

- Dates of service
- Final rank awarded

- Duties and responsibilities
- All citations and awards
- Details on specific training and/or special schooling
- Skills developed
- Specific accomplishments

Creating Your First Resume

There are a lot of options about what to include or leave out. In general, we suggest you always include the following data:

- Your name, address and telephone number
- Pertinent educational history (grades, class rank, activities, etc.)
- Pertinent work history
- Academic honors
- Memberships in organizations
- Military service history (if applicable)

You have the option of including the following:

- Your career objective
- Personal data
- Hobbies
- Summary of qualifications

And you should *never* include the following:

- Photographs or illustrations (of yourself or anything else) unless they are required by your profession—e.g., actors' composites
- Why you left past jobs
- References
- Salary history or present salary objectives/requirements (if salary history is requested in an ad, include it in your cover letter)
- Feelings about travel or relocation

Special note: There is definitely a school of thought that discourages any mention of personal data—marital status, health, etc.—on a resume. While I am not vehemently opposed to including such information, I am not convinced it is particularly necessary, either.

As far as hobbies go, I would only include such information if it were in some way pertinent to the job/career you're targeting. Your love of reading is pertinent if, for example, you are applying for a part-time job at a library. But including details on the joys of "hiking, long walks with my dog and Isaac Asimov short stories" is rarely correct.

Maximizing Form And Substance

Your resume should be limited to a single page if possible, two at most. When you're laying out the resume, try to leave a reasonable amount of "white space"—generous margins all around and spacing between entries. It should be typed or printed (not Xeroxed) on 8 1/2" x 11" white, cream or ivory stock. The ink should be black or, at most, a royal blue.

Don't scrimp on the paper quality—use the best bond you can afford. And since printing 100 or even 200 copies will cost little more than 50, if you do decide to print your resume, *over*estimate your needs, and opt for the highest quantity you think you may need. Prices at various "quick print" shops are not exorbitant; the quality look printing affords will leave the right impression.

Use Power Words For Impact

Be brief. Use phraseology rather than complete sentences. Your resume is a summary of your talents, not a term paper. Choose your words carefully and use "power words" whenever possible. "Organized" is more powerful than "put together;" "supervised" better than "oversaw;" "formulated" better than "thought up."

Strong words like these can make the most mundane clerical work sound like a series of responsible, professional positions. And, of course, they will tend to make your resume stand out. Here's a starter list of words that you may want to use in your resume:

achieved	administered	advised
analyzed	applied	arranged
budgeted	calculated	classified
communicated	completed	computed
conceptualized	coordinated	critiqued
delegated	determined	developed
devised	directed	established
evaluated	executed	formulated
gathered	generated	guided
implemented	improved	initiated
instituted	instructed	introduced
invented	issued	launched
lectured	litigated	lobbied
managed	negotiated	operated
organized	overhauled	planned
prepared	presented	presided
programmed	promoted	recommended
researched	reviewed	revised
reorganized	regulated	selected
solved	scheduled	supervised
systematized	taught	tested
trained	updated	utilized

Choose The Right Format

There is not a lot of mystery here—your background will generally lead you to the right format. For an entry-level job applicant with limited work experience, the **chronological** format, which organizes your educational and employment history by date (most recent first) is the obvious choice.

For older or more experienced applicants, either the **functional**—which emphasizes the duties and responsibilities of all your jobs over the course of your career—or **combination**—halfway between chronological and functional—may be more suitable. While I have tended to emphasize the chronological format in this chapter, one of the other two may well be the right one for you.

Here's What To Avoid

In case we didn't stress them enough, here are some reminders of what to avoid:

- **Be brief and to the point**—Two pages if absolutely necessary, one page if at all possible. Never longer!

- **Don't be fancy.** Multi-colored paper and all-italic type won't impress employers, just make your resume harder to read (and easier to discard). Use plain white or ivory paper, blue or black ink and an easy-to-read standard typeface.

- **Forget rules about sentences.** Say what you need to say in the fewest words possible; use phrases, not drawn-out sentences.

- **Stick to the facts.** Don't talk about your dog, vacation, etc.

- **Resumes should never be blind.** A cover letter should *always* accompany a resume and that letter should always be directed to a specific person.

- **Almost doesn't count.** Your resume *must* be perfect—proofread everything as many times as necessary to catch any misspellings, grammatical errors, strange hyphenations or typos.

- **This is your sales tool.** Your resume is, in many cases, as close to you as an employer will ever get. Make sure it includes the information necessary to sell yourself the way you want to be sold!

- **Spend the money for good printing.** Soiled, tattered or poorly reproduced copies speak poorly of your own self-image. Spend the money and take the time to make sure your resume is the best presentation you've ever made.

- **Help the reader,** by organizing your resume in a clear-cut manner so key points are easily gleaned.

On pages 106 to 119, we have prepared eight *Data Input Sheets*. The first six cover employment, volunteer work, education, activities and awards and are essential to any resume. The last two—covering military service and language skills—are important if, of course, they apply to you. I've included multiple copies of the employment and volunteer sheets, but only one each of the others. If you need to, you can copy the forms you need (or write up your own using these models).

Employment Data Input Sheet: You will need to record the basic information—employer's name, address and phone number, dates of employment and your supervisor's name—for your own files anyway. It may be an important addition to your networking list and will be necessary should you be asked to supply a reference list.

Duties should be a one- or two-sentence paragraph describing what you did on this job. For example, if you worked as a hostess in a restaurant, this section might read: "Responsible for the delivery of 250 meals at dinner time and the supervision of 20 waiters and busboys. Coordinated reservations. Responsible for check and payment verification."

Skills should enumerate specific capabilities necessary for the job or developed through it.

If you achieved *specific results*—e.g., "developed new filing system," "collected over $5,000 in previously-assumed bad debt," "instituted award-winning art program," etc.—or *received any award, citation or other honor*—"named Employee of the Month three times," "received Mayor's Citation for Innovation," etc.—make sure you list these.

Prepare one Employment Data Sheet for each job you have held, no matter how short the job (yes, summer jobs count) or how limited you may think it is.

Volunteer Work Data Input Sheet: Treat any volunteer work, no matter how basic or short (one day counts!), as if it were a job and record the same information. In both cases, it is especially important to note specific duties and responsibilities, skills required or developed and any accomplishments or achievements you can point to as evidence of your success.

Educational Data Input Sheet: If you're in college, omit details on high school. If you're a graduate student, list details on both graduate and undergraduate coursework. If you have not yet graduated, list your anticipated date of graduation. If more than a year away, indicate the numbers of credits earned through the most recent semester to be completed.

Activities Data Input Sheet: This is where to list your participation in the Student Government, Winter Carnival Press Committee, Math Club, Ski Patrol, etc., plus sports teams and/or any participation in community or church groups. Make sure you indicate if you were elected to any positions in clubs, groups or on teams.

Awards And Honors Data Input Sheet: List awards and honors from your school (prestigious high school awards can still be included here, even if you're in graduate school), community groups, church groups, clubs, etc.

Military Service Data Input Sheet: Many useful skills are learned in the armed forces. A military stint often hastens the maturation process, making you a more attractive candidate. So if you have served in the military, make sure you include details in your resume.

Language Data Input Sheet: An extremely important section for those of you with a real proficiency in a second language. And *do* make sure you have at least conversational fluency in the language(s) you list. One year of college French doesn't count, but if you've studied abroad, you probably are fluent or near-fluent. Such a talent could be invaluable, especially if you hope to work in the international arena.

While you should use the following forms to summarize all of the data you have collected, do not throw away any of the specific information—report cards, transcripts, citations, etc.—just because it is recorded on these sheets. Keep *all* records in your files; you'll never know when you'll need them again!

You can then use the information you have collected to construct your own resume using the "fill-in-the-blanks" form on pages 120 to 125.

Employment Data Input Sheet

Employer name: _____

Address: _____

Address: _____

Phone: _____   Dates of Employment: _____

Hours Per Week: _____   Salary/Pay: _____

Supervisor's Name & Title: _____

Duties: _____

_____

_____

Skills Utilized: _____

_____

_____

_____

_____

_____

Accomplishments/Honors/Awards: _____

_____

_____

_____

Other Important Information: _____

_____

_____

_____

_____

Employment Data Input Sheet

Employer name: _____

Address: _____

Address: _____

Phone: _____ Dates of Employment: _____

Hours Per Week: _____ Salary/Pay: _____

Supervisor's Name & Title: _____

Duties: _____

_____

_____

Skills Utilized: _____

_____

_____

_____

_____

_____

Accomplishments/Honors/Awards: _____

_____

_____

_____

Other Important Information: _____

_____

_____

_____

_____

Employment Data Input Sheet

Employer name: _____

Address: _____

Address: _____

Phone: _____ Dates of Employment: _____

Hours Per Week: _____ Salary/Pay: _____

Supervisor's Name & Title: _____

Duties: _____

_____

_____

Skills Utilized: _____

_____

_____

_____

_____

Accomplishments/Honors/Awards: _____

_____

_____

_____

Other Important Information: _____

_____

_____

_____

_____

Employment Data Input Sheet

Employer name: _____

Address: _____

Address: _____

Phone: _____   Dates of Employment: _____

Hours Per Week: _____   Salary/Pay: _____

Supervisor's Name & Title: _____

Duties: _____

_____

_____

Skills Utilized: _____

_____

_____

_____

_____

_____

Accomplishments/Honors/Awards: _____

_____

_____

_____

Other Important Information: _____

_____

_____

_____

_____

Employment Data Input Sheet

Employer name: _____

Address: _____

Address: _____

Phone: _____   Dates of Employment: _____

Hours Per Week: _____   Salary/Pay: _____

Supervisor's Name & Title: _____

Duties: _____

_____

_____

Skills Utilized: _____

_____

_____

_____

_____

_____

Accomplishments/Honors/Awards: _____

_____

_____

_____

Other Important Information: _____

_____

_____

_____

_____

Volunteer Work Data Input Sheet

Organization name: _____

Address: _____

Address: _____ Phone: _____

Hours Per Week: _____ Dates of Activity: _____

Supervisor's Name & Title: _____

Duties: _____

_____

_____

Skills Utilized: _____

_____

_____

_____

_____

Accomplishments/Honors/Awards: _____

_____

_____

_____

_____

Other Important Information: _____

_____

_____

_____

_____

_____

Volunteer Work Data Input Sheet

Organization name: _____

Address: _____

Address: _____ Phone: _____

Hours Per Week: _____ Dates of Activity: _____

Supervisor's Name & Title: _____

Duties: _____

_____

_____

Skills Utilized: _____

_____

_____

_____

_____

Accomplishments/Holors/Awards: _____

_____

_____

_____

_____

Other Important Information: _____

_____

_____

_____

_____

_____

Volunteer Work Data Input Sheet

Organization name: _____

Address: _____

Address: _____ Phone: _____

Hours Per Week: _____ Dates of Activity: _____

Supervisor's Name & Title: _____

Duties: _____

_____

_____

Skills Utilized: _____

_____

_____

_____

_____

Accomplishments/Honors/Awards: _____

_____

_____

_____

_____

Other Important Information: _____

_____

_____

_____

_____

_____

High School Data Input Sheet

School name: _____

Address: _____

Phone: _____ Years Attended: _____

Major Studies: _____

GPA/Class Rank: _____

Honors: _____

Important Courses: _____

_____

_____

_____

_____

_____

Other School Data Input Sheet

School name: _____

Address: _____

Phone: _____ Years Attended: _____

Major Studies: _____ GPA/Class Rank: _____

Honors: _____

Important Courses: _____

_____

_____

_____

College Data Input Sheet

College: _____

Address: _____

Phone: _____ Years Attended: _____

Degrees Earned: _____ Major: _____ Minor: _____

Honors: _____

_____

Important Courses: _____

_____

_____

_____

_____

Graduate School Data Input Sheet

College: _____

Address: _____

Phone: _____ Years Attended: _____

Degrees Earned: _____ Major: _____ Minor: _____

Honors: _____

_____

Important Courses: _____

_____

_____

_____

Activities Data Input Sheet

Club/Activity: _____ Office(s) held: _____

Description of participation: _____

_____

Duties/Responsibilities: _____

_____

_____

Club/Activity: _____ Office(s) held: _____

Description of participation: _____

_____

Duties/Responsibilities: _____

_____

_____

Club/Activity: _____ Office(s) held: _____

Description of participation: _____

_____

Duties/Responsibilities: _____

_____

_____

Club/Activity: _____ Office(s) held: _____

Description of participation: _____

_____

Duties/Responsibilities: _____

_____

_____

Awards & Honors Data Input Sheet

Name of Award, Citation, Etc.: _____

From Whom Received: _____ Date: _____

Significance: _____

_____

_____

Other pertinent information: _____

_____

_____

Name of Award, Citation, Etc.: _____

From Whom Received: _____ Date: _____

Significance: _____

_____

_____

Other pertinent information: _____

_____

_____

Name of Award, Citation, Etc.: _____

From Whom Received: _____ Date: _____

Significance: _____

_____

_____

Other pertinent information: _____

_____

_____

Military Service Data Input Sheet

Branch: _____

Rank (at Discharge): _____

Dates of Service: _____

Duties & Responsibilities: _____

_____

_____

_____

_____

Special Training and/or School Attended: _____

_____

_____

_____

_____

Citations, Awards, etc.: _____

_____

_____

_____

Specific Accomplishments: _____

_____

_____

_____

_____

_____

Language Data Input Sheet

Language: _____

☐ Read   ☐ Write   ☐ Converse

Background (number of years studied, travel, etc.): _____

_____

_____

_____

_____

_____

Language: _____

☐ Read   ☐ Write   ☐ Converse

Background : _____

_____

_____

_____

_____

_____

Language: _____

☐ Read   ☐ Write   ☐ Converse

Background : _____

_____

_____

_____

_____

_____

Fill-In-The-Blanks Resume Form

Name : _____

Address : _____

City, state, zip code : _____

Telephone number : _____

OBJECTIVE :_____

_____

_____

_____

SUMMARY OF QUALIFICATIONS: _____

_____

_____

_____

_____

_____

_____

EDUCATION:

Graduate School : _____

Address : _____

Address: _____

Expected graduation date : _____   Grade point average : _____

Degree earned (expected): _____   Class rank : _____

Important classes you have taken, especially those that relate to your targeted career:

_____

_____

_____

_____

_____

_____

COLLEGE:_____

Address : _____

Address: _____

Expected graduation date : _____Grade point average : _____

Class rank : _____ Major:_____ Minor: _____

Important classes you have taken, especially those that relate to your expected career:

_____

_____

_____

_____

_____

_____

_____

_____

HIGH SCHOOL:_____

Address : _____

Address: _____

Expected graduation date : _____Grade point average : _____

Class rank : _____

Important classes you have taken, especially those that relate to your expected career:

_____

_____

_____

_____

_____

_____

_____

HOBBIES AND OTHER INTERESTS (OPTIONAL)

_____

_____

_____

_____

_____

_____

_____

_____

EXTRACURRICULAR ACTIVITIES (Activity name, dates participated, duties and responsibilities, offices held, accomplishments):

_____

_____

_____

_____

_____

_____

_____

_____

AWARDS AND HONORS (Award name, from whom and date received, significance of the award, any other pertinent details):

_____

_____

_____

_____

_____

_____

WORK EXPERIENCE Include job title, name of business, address and phone number, dates of employment, supervisor's name and title, your major responsibilities, accomplishments and any awards won. Include volunteer experience in this category. List your experiences with the most recent dates first, even if you later decide not to use a chronological format

_____

_____

_____

_____

_____

_____

_____

_____

_____

_____

_____

_____

_____

_____

_____

_____

_____

_____

REFERENCES Though you should *not* include references in your resume, you do need to prepare a separate list of at least three people who know you fairly well and will, you believe, recommend you highly to prospective employers. For each, include job title, company name, address and telephone number. Before you include anyone on this list, make sure you have their permission to use their name as a reference and confirm what they intend to say about you to a potential employer.

1. _____

_____

_____

_____

2. _____

_____

_____

_____

3. _____

_____

_____

_____

4. _____

_____

_____

_____

5. _____

_____

_____

_____

6. _____

_____

_____

_____

19

Writing Better Letters

Stop for a moment and review your resume draft. It is undoubtedly (by now) a near-perfect document that instantly tells the reader the kind of job you want and why you are qualified. But does it say anything personal about you? Any amplification of your talents? Any words that are ideally "you?" Any hint of the kind of person who stands behind that resume?

If you've prepared it properly, the answers should be a series of ringing "no's"—your resume should be a mere sketch of your life, a bare-bones summary of your skills, education and experience.

To the general we must add the specific. That's what your letters must accomplish—adding the lines, colors and shading that will help fill out your self portrait. This chapter will cover the kinds of letters you will most often be called upon to prepare in your job search. There are essentially nine different types you will utilize again and again, based primarily on what each is trying to accomplish. I've included at least one well-written example of each at the end of this chapter.

Before you put pencil to paper to compose any letter, there are five key questions you must ask yourself:

- **Why** are you writing it?
- To **Whom?**
- **What** are you trying to accomplish?.
- **Which** lead will get the reader's attention?
- **How** do you organize the letter to best accomplish your objectives?

Why?

There should be a single, easily-definable reason you are writing any letter. This reason will often dictate what and how you write—the tone and flavor of the letter—as well as what you include or leave out.

Have you been asked in an ad to amplify your qualifications for a job, provide a salary history and college transcripts? Then that (minimally) is your objective in writing. Limit yourself to following instructions and do a little personal selling—but very little. Including everything asked for and a simple, adequate cover letter is better than writing a "knock-'em, sock-'em" letter and omitting your salary history.

If, however, you are on a networking search, the objective of your letter is to seek out contacts who will refer you for possible informational or job interviews. In this case, getting a name and address—a referral—is your stated purpose for writing. You have to be specific and ask for this action.

You will no doubt follow up with a phone call, but be certain the letter conveys what you are after. Being vague or oblique won't help you. You are after a definite yes or no when it comes to contact assistance. The recipient of your letter should know this. As they say in the world of selling, at some point you have to ask for the order.

Who?

Using the proper "tone" in a letter is as important as the content—you wouldn't write a letter to your television repairman using the same words and style you would employ in a letter to the director of personnel of a major TV station. Properly addressing the person or persons you are writing is as important as what you say to them.

Some hints to utilize: the recipient's job title and level, his or her hiring clout (if they are just a pass along conduit, save your selling for the next step up the ladder), the kind of person they are (based on your knowledge of their area of involvement).

For example, it pays to sound technical with technical people—in other words, use the kinds of words and language which they use on the job. If you have had the opportunity to speak with them, it will be easy for you. If not, and you have formed some opinions as to their types then use these as the basis of the language you employ. The cardinal rule is to say it in words you think the recipient will be comfortable hearing, not in the words you might otherwise personally choose.

What?

What do you have to offer that station? What do you have to contribute to the job, process or work situation that is unique and/or of particular benefit to the recipient of your letter?

For example, if you were applying for a time sales position and recently ranked number one in a summer sales job, then conveying this benefit is logical and desirable. It is a factor you may have left off your resume. Even if it was listed in your skills/accomplishment section of the resume, you can underscore and call attention to it in your letter. Repetition, when it is properly focused, can be a good thing.

Which?

Of all the opening sentences you can compose, which will immediately get the reader's attention? If your opening sentence is dynamic, you are already fifty percent of the way to your end objective—having your entire letter read. Don't slide into it. Know the point you are trying to make and come right to it.

How?

While a good opening is essential, how do you organize your letter so that it is easy for the recipient to read in its entirety? This is a question of *flow*—the way the words and sentences naturally lead one to another, holding the reader's interest until he or she reaches your signature.

If you have your objective clearly in mind, this task is easier than it sounds: Simply convey your message(s) in a logical sequence. End your letter by stating what the next steps are—yours and/or the reader's.

One More Time

Pay attention to the small things. Neatness still counts. Have your letters typed. Spend a few extra dollars and have some personal stationary printed.

And most important, make certain that your correspondence goes out quickly. The general rule is to get a letter in the mail during the week in which the project comes to your attention or in which you have had some contact with the organization. I personally attempt to mail follow-up letters the same day as the contact; at worst, within 24 hours.

When To Write

- To answer an ad
- To prospect (many companies)
- To inquire about specific openings (single company)
- To obtain a referral
- To obtain an informational interview
- To obtain a job interview
- To say "thank you"
- To accept or reject a job offer
- To withdraw from consideration for a job

In some cases, the letter will accompany your resume; in others, it will need to stand alone. Each of the above circumstance is described in the pages that follow. I have included at least one sample of each type of letter at the end of this chapter.

Answering An Ad

Your eye catches an ad in the Positions Available Section of the Sunday paper for a production assistant. It tells you that the position is in a large metropolitan TV station and that, though some experience would be desirable, it is not required. Well, you possess *those* skills. The ad asks that you send a letter and resume to a Post Office Box. No salary is indicated, no phone number given. You decide to reply.

Your purpose in writing—the objective (why?)—is to secure a job interview. Since no individual is singled out for receipt of the ad, and since it is a large station, you assume it will be screened by Personnel.

Adopt a professional, formal tone. You are answering a "blind" ad, so you have to play it safe. In your first sentence, refer to the ad—including the place and date of publication and the position outlined. (Chances are this hospital is running more than one ad on the same date and in the same paper, so you need to identify the one to which you are replying.) Tell the reader what (specifically) you have to offer that station. Include your resume, phone number and the times it is easiest to reach you. Ask for the order—tell them you'd like to have an appointment.

Blanket Prospecting Letter

In June of this year you will graduate with your Communications degree. You seek an entry-level reporting position at a mid-sized TV station. You have decided to write to fifty stations in the areas you would like to work, sending each a copy of your resume. You don't know which, if any, have job openings.

Such blanket mailings are effective given two circumstances: 1) You must have an exemplary record and a resume which reflects it, and 2) You must send out a goodly number of packages, since the response rate to such mailings is very low.

A blanket mailing doesn't mean an impersonal one—you should *always* be writing to a specific executive. If you have a referral, send a personalized letter to that person. If not, do *not* simply mail a package to the Personnel department; identify the department head and *then* send a personalized letter. And make sure you get on the phone and follow up each letter within about ten days. Don't just sit back and wait for everyone to call you. They won't.

Just Inquiring

The inquiry letter is a step above the blanket prospecting letter; it's a "cold-calling" device with a twist. You have earmarked a facility (and a person) as a possibility in your job search based on something you have read about them. Your general research tells you that it is a good place to work. Although you are not aware of any specific openings, you know that they employ entry-level personnel with your credentials.

While ostensibly inquiring about any openings, you are really just "referring yourself" to them in order to place your resume in front of the right person. This is what I would call a "why not?" attempt at securing a job interview. Its effectiveness depends on their actually having been in the news. This, after all, is your "excuse" for writing.

Networking

It's time to get out that folder marked "Contacts" and prepare a draft networking letter. The lead sentence should be very specific, referring immediately to the friend, colleague, etc. "who suggested I write you about..." Remember: Your objective is to secure an informational interview, pave the way for a job interview, and/or get referred to still other contacts.

This type of letter should not place the recipient in a position where a decision is necessary; rather, the request should be couched in terms of "career advice." The second paragraph can then inform the reader of your level of experience. Finally, be specific about seeking an appointment.

Unless you have been specifically asked by the referring person to do so, you will probably not be including a resume with such letters. So the letter itself must highlight your credentials, enabling the reader to gauge your relative level of experience. For entry-level personnel, education, of course, will be most important.

For An Informational Interview

Though the objectives of this letter are similar to those of the networking letter, they are not as personal. These are "knowledge quests" on your part and the recipient will most likely not be someone you have been referred to. The idea is to convince the reader of the sincerity of your research effort. Whatever selling you do, if you do any at all, will arise as a consequence of the meeting, not beforehand.

A positive response to this type of request is in itself a good step forward. It is, after all, exposure, and amazing things can develop when people in authority agree to see you.

Thank-You Letters

Although it may not always seem so, manners *do* count in the job world. But what counts even more are the simple gestures that show you actually care—like writing a thank-you letter. A well-executed, timely thank-you note tells more about your personality than anything else you may have sent. It says something about the way you were brought up—whatever else your resume tells them, you are, at least, polite, courteous and thoughtful.

Thank-you letters may well become the beginning of an all-important dialogue that leads directly to a job. So be extra careful in composing them, and make certain that they are custom made for each occasion and person.

The following are the primary situations in which you will be called upon to write some variation of thank-you letter:

- After a job interview

- After an informational interview

- Accepting a job offer

- Responding to rejection: While optional, such a letter is appropriate if you have been among the finalists in a job search or were rejected due to limited experience. Remember: Some day you'll *have* enough experience; make the interviewer want to stay in touch.

- Withdrawing from consideration: Used when you decide you are no longer interested in a particular position. (A variation is usable for declining an actual job offer.) Whatever the reason for writing such a letter, it's wise to do so and thus keep future lines of communication open.

In Response To An Ad

10 E. 89th Street
New York, N.Y. 10028
December 3, 1991

The <u>New York Times</u>
P.O. Box 7520
New York, N.Y. 10128

Dear Sir or Madam:

This letter is in response to your advertisement for a production assistant which appeared in the December 2nd issue of the *New York Times*.

I have the qualifications you are seeking. I graduated with a 3.8 grade point average (A = 4.0) from Boola Boola Community College with a major in television production and a minor in communications.

I also completed a six-month certificate program at Ace Technical Institute and have worked part-time throughout college at the local television station in a variety of clerical and assistant positions.

My resume is enclosed. I would like to have the opportunity to meet with you personally to discuss your requirements for the position. I can be reached at (212) 785-1225 between 8:00 a.m. and 5:00 p.m. and at (212) 785-4221 after 5:00 p.m. I look forward to hearing from you.

Sincerely,

Karen Weber

Enclosure: Resume, Clips

Prospecting Letter

Kim Kerr
8 Robutuck Hwy.
Hammond, IN 54054
555-875-2392

December 14, 1991

Ms. Carol Edgar Jones
Director-Recruitment
Chicago Broadcasting Company
One Lakeshore Drive
Chicago, Illinois

Dear Ms. Jones:

The name of CBC continually pops up in our classroom discussions of outstanding broadcasting companies. Given my interest in broadcasting as a career and reporting as a specialty, I've taken the liberty of enclosing my resume.

As you can see, I have just completed my Bachelor's degree in Communications at Wright University. Though my resume does not indicate it, I will be graduating in the top 10% of my class, with honors.

I have wanted to be a reporter since I was a little girl. To make sure my "dream" matched "reality," I have worked at a variety of radio and television stations since high school—summers, after school, vacations—in a wide variety of positions.

I will be in the Chicago area on January 5 and will call your office to see when it is convenient to arrange an appointment.

Sincerely yours,

Kim Kerr

Inquiry Letter

42 7th Street
Ski City, Vermont 85722
September 30, 1991

Ms. Crystal Igotmine
President
Really Big Antenna, Inc.
521 West Elm Street
Indianapolis, IN 83230

Dear Ms. Igotmine:

I just completed reading the article in the October issue of <u>Fortune</u> on your company's record-breaking quarter. Congratulations!

Your innovative approach to recruiting minorities is of particular interest to me because of my background in advertising and minority recruitment.

I am interested in learning more about your work as well as the possibilities of joining your firm. My qualifications include:

- B.A. in Psychology
- Research on minority recruitment
- Publicity Seminar participation (Univ. of Virginia)
- Reports preparation on creative writing, education and minorities

I will be in Indianapolis during the week of October 10 and hope your schedule will permit us to meet briefly to discuss our mutual interests. I will call your mffice next week to see if such a meeting can be arranged.

I appreciate your consideration.

Sincerely yours,

Ronald W. Sodidie

Networking Letter

Richard A. Starky
42 Bach St., Musical City, IN 20202   **317-555-1515**

May 14, 1991

Ms. Michelle Fleming
Vice President-Sales
Small Station, Inc.
42 Jenkins Avenue
Fulton, Mississippi 23232

Dear Ms. Fleming:

Ed Wallace suggested I write you. I am interested in an entry-level sales position, but <u>not</u> at a large station. Ed felt it would be mutually beneficial for us to meet and talk.

I have four years of sterling sales results to boast of, experience acquired while working my way through college. I believe my familiarity with retail sales and Bachelor's degree in marketing from American University have properly prepared me for a career in broadcast sales.

As I begin my job search during the next few months, I am certain your advice would help me. Would it be possible for us to meet briefly? My resume is enclosed.

I will call your office next week to see when your schedule would permit such a meeting.

Sincerely,

Richard A. Starky

Enc: Resume

To Obtain An Informational Interview

16 NW 128th Street
Raleigh, North Carolina 75755
December 2, 1991

Ms. Michelle Fleming
Vice President-Sales
THE Network
42 Jenkins Avenue
Fulton, Mississippi 23232

Dear Ms. Fleming:

I'm sure a great deal of the credit for your outstanding sales gain in the fourth quarter were due to your innovative time sales training program. Congratulations on your division's record-shattering performance.

I have four years of sterling sales results to boast of, experience acquired while working my way through college. I believe my familiarity with the broadcast industry, sales experience and Bachelor's degree in communications from American University have properly prepared me for a career in television time sales.

As I begin my job search, I am trying to gather as much information and advice as possible before applying for positions. Could I take a few minutes of your time next week to discuss my career plans? I will call your office on Monday, December 12, to see if such a meeting can be arranged.

I appreciate your consideration and look forward to meeting you.

Sincerely,

Karen R. Burns

After An Informational Interview

LAZELLE WRIGHT
921 West Fourth Street
Steamboat, Colorado 72105
303-303-3030

May 21, 1991

Mr. James R. Payne
Recruitment Manager
THE Network
241 Snowridge
Ogden, Utah 72108

Dear Mr. Payne:

Jinny Bastienelli was right when she said you would be most helpful in advising me on a career in television news.

I appreciated your taking the time from your busy schedule to meet with me. Your advice was most helpful and I have incorporated your suggestions into my resume. I will send you a copy next week.

Again, thanks so much for your assistance. As you suggested, I will contact Joe Simmons at K-BRP next week in regards to a possible opening with his station.

Sincerely,

Lazelle Wright

After A Job Interview

1497 Lilac Street
Old Adams, MA 01281
October 5, 1991

Mr. Rudy Delacort
Director of Personnel
WII-AM
175 Boylston Avenue
Ribbit, Massachusetts 02857

Dear Mr. Delacort:

Thank you for the opportunity to interview yesterday for the time sales trainee position. I enjoyed meeting you and Cliff Stoudt and learning more about WII.

Your organization appears to be growing in a direction which parallels my interests and career goals. The interview with you and your staff confirmed my initial positive impressions of WII, and I want to reiterate my strong interest in working for you.

I am convinced my prior experience as ad sales director for my school's daily newspaper, my Business College training in marketing and finance, and my summer sales experience working with a variety of products would enable me to progress steadily through your training program and become a productive member of your sales team.

Again, thank you for your consideration. If you need any additional information from me, please feel free to call.

Yours truly,

Hugh Beaumont

cc: Mr. Cliff Stoudt
      Sales Training Manager

Accepting A Job Offer

1497 Lilac Street
Old Adams, MA 01281
October 5, 1991

Mr. Rudy Delacort
Director of Personnel
WII-AM
175 Boylston Avenue
Ribbit, Massachusetts 02857

Dear Mr. Delacort:

I want to thank you and Mr. Stoudt for giving me the opportunity to work for WII. I am very pleased to accept the position as a sales rep trainee. The position entails exactly the kind of work I want to do, and I know that I will do a good job for you.

As we discussed, I shall begin work on January 5, 1992. In the interim I shall complete all the necessary employment forms, obtain the required physical examination and locate housing.

I plan to be in Ribbit within the next two weeks and would like to deliver the paperwork to you personally. At that time, we could handle any remaining items pertaining to my employment. I'll call next week to schedule an appointment with you.

Sincerely yours,

Edward J. Haskell

cc: Mr. Cliff Stoudt
    Sales Training Manager

Withdrawing From Consideration

1497 Lilac Street
Old Adams, MA 01281
October 5, 1991

Mr. Rudy Delacort
Director of Personnel
WII-AM
175 Boylston Avenue
Ribbit, Massachusetts 02857

Dear Mr. Delacort:

It was indeed a pleasure meeting with you and Mr. Stoudt last week to discuss your needs for a sales rep trainee. Our time together was most enjoyable and informative.

As I discussed with you during our meetings, I believe one purpose of preliminary interviews is to explore areas of mutual interest and to assess the fit between the individual and the position. After careful consideration, I have decided to withdraw from consideration for the position.

My decision is based primarily upon the one factor we discussed in some detail—the position would simply require more travel than I am able to accept, given my other responsibilities.

I want to thank you for interviewing me and giving me the opportunity to learn about your needs. You have a fine staff and and I would have enjoyed working with them.

Yours truly,

Barbara Billingsly

cc: Mr. Cliff Stoudt
    Sales Training Manager

In Response To Rejection

1497 Lilac Street
Old Adams, MA 01281
October 5, 1991

Mr. Rudy Delacort
Director of Personnel
WII-AM
175 Boylston Avenue
Ribbit, Massachusetts   02857

Dear Mr. Delacort:

Thank you for giving me the opportunity to interview for the sales rep trainee position. I appreciate your consideration and interest in me.

Although I am disappointed in not being selected for your current vacancy, I want you to know that I appreciated the courtesy and professionalism shown to me during the entire selection process. I enjoyed meeting you, Cliff Stoudt, and the other members of your sales staff. My meetings confirmed that WII would be an exciting place to work and build a career.

I want to reiterate my strong interest in working for you. Please keep me in mind if a similar position becomes available in the near future.

Again, thank you for the opportunity to interview and best wishes to you and your staff.

Sincerely yours,

Anthony Dow

cc: Mr. Cliff Stoudt
    Sales Training Manager

20

Questions For You, Questions For Them

You've done days of research, contacted everyone you've known since kindergarten, compiled a professional-looking and -sounding resume, and written brilliant letters to the handful of companies your research has revealed are perfect matches for your own strengths, interests and abilities. Unfortunately, all of this preparatory work will be meaningless if you are unable to successfully convince one of those firms to hire you.

If you were able set up an initial meeting at one of these companies, your resume and cover letter obviously peaked *someone's* interest. Now you have to traverse the last minefield—the job interview itself. It's time to make all that preparation pay off.

This chapter will attempt to put the interview process in perspective, giving you the "inside story" on what to expect and how to handle the questions and circumstances that arise during the course of a normal interview...and even many of those that surface in the bizarre interview situations we have all sometimes experienced.

Why Interviews Shouldn't Scare You

Interviews shouldn't scare you. The concept of two (or more) persons meeting to determine if they are right for each other is a relatively logical and certainly not apparently frightening idea. As important as research, resumes, letters and phone calls are, they are inherently impersonal. The interview is your chance to really see and feel the company firsthand—"up close and personal," as Howard Cosell used to crow—so think of it as a positive opportunity, your chance to succeed.

That said, many of you will still be put off by the inherently inquisitive nature of the process. Though many questions *will* be asked, interviews are essentially experiments in chemistry. Are you right for the company? Is the company right for you? Not just on paper—*in the flesh*. If you decide the company *is* right for you, *your* purpose is simple and clearcut—to convince the interviewer that you are the right person for the job, that you will fit in, and that you will be an asset to the company now and in the future. The interviewer's purpose is equally simple—to decide whether he or she should buy what you're selling.

This chapter will focus on the kinds of questions you are likely to be asked, how to answer them, and the questions you should be ready to ask of the interviewer. By removing the workings of the interview process from the "unknown" category, you will reduce the fear it engenders.

But all the preparation in the world won't completely eliminate your sweaty palms, unless you can convince yourself that the interview is an important, positive life experience from which you will benefit...even if you don't get the job. Approach it with a little enthusiasm, calm yourself, and let your personality do the rest. You will undoubtedly spend an interesting hour, one that will teach you more about yourself. It's just another step in the learning process you've undertaken.

What To Do First

Start by setting up a calendar on which you can enter and track all your scheduled appointments. When you schedule an interview with a company, ask them how much time you should allow for the appointment. Some require all new applicants to fill out numerous forms and/or complete a battery of intelligence or psychological tests—all before the first interview. If you've only allowed an hour for the interview—and scheduled another at a nearby firm ten minutes later—the first time you confront a three-hour test series will effectively destroy any schedule.

Some companies, especially if the first interview is very positive, like to keep applicants around to talk to other executives. This process may be planned or, in a lot of cases, a spontaneous decision by an interviewer who likes you and wants you to meet some other key decision makers. Other companies will tend to schedule such a series of second interviews on a separate day. Find out, if you can, how the company you're planning to visit generally operates. Otherwise, especially if you've traveled to another city to interview with a number of firms in a short period of time, a schedule that's too tight will fall apart in no time at all.

If you need to travel out-of-state to interview with a company, be sure to ask if they will be paying some or all of your travel expenses. (It's generally expected that you'll be paying your own way to firms within your home state.) If they don't offer—and you don't ask—presume you're paying the freight.

Even if the company agrees to reimburse you, make sure you have enough money to pay all the expenses yourself. While some may reimburse you immediately, the majority of firms may take from a week to a month to forward you an expense check.

What Color Shirts Does He Like?

The research you did to find these companies is nothing compared to the research you need to do now that you're beginning to narrow your search. If you followed our detailed suggestions when you started targeting these firms in the first place, you've already amassed a lot of information about them. If you didn't do the research *then*, you sure better decide to do it *now*. Study each company as if you were going to be tested on your detailed knowledge of their organization and operations. Here's what you should know about each company you plan to visit:

The Basics

1. The address of (and directions to) the office you're visiting
2. Headquarters location (if different)
3. Some idea of domestic and international branches
4. Relative size (compared to other similar companies)
5. Annual billings, sales and/or income (last two years)

6. Subsidiary companies; specialized divisions
7. Departments (overall structure)
8. Major accounts, products or services

The Subtleties

1. History of the firm (specialties, honors, awards, famous names)
2. Names, titles and backgrounds of top management
3. Existence (and type) of training program
4. Relocation policy
5. Relative salaries (compared to other companies in field or by size)
6. Recent developments concerning the the company and its products or services (from your trade magazine and newspaper reading)
7. Everything you can learn about the career, likes and dislikes of the person(s) interviewing you

The amount of time and work necessary to be *this* well prepared for an interview is considerable. It will not be accomplished the day before the interview. You may even find some of the information you need to be unavailable on short notice.

(Is it really so important to do all this? Well, **somebody out there is going to.** *And if you happen to be interviewing for the same job as that other, well-prepared, knowledgeable candidate, who do* **you** *think will impress the interviewer more?)*

As we've already discussed, if you give yourself enough time, most of this information is surprisingly easy to obtain. In addition to the reference sources we previously covered (see Appendix B, too), the company itself can probably supply you with a great deal of data. A firm's annual report—which all publicly-owned companies must publish yearly for their stockholders—is a virtual treasure trove of information. Write each company and request copies of their last two annual reports. A comparison of sales, income and other data over this period may enable you to discover some interesting things about their overall financial health and growth potential. Many libraries also have collections of annual reports from major corporations.

Attempting to learn about your interviewer is a chore, the importance of which is underestimated by most applicants (who then, of course, don't bother to do it). Being one of the exceptions may get you a job. Use the biographical references available in your local library. If he or she is listed in any of these sources, you'll be able to learn an awful lot about his or her background. In addition, find out if he or she has written any articles that have appeared in the trade press or, even better, books on his or her area(s) of expertise. Referring to these writings during the course of an interview, without making it *too* obvious a compliment, can be very effective. We all have egos and we all like people to talk about us. The interviewer is no different from the rest of us. You might also check to see if any of your networking contacts worked with him or her at his current (or a previous) company and can help "fill you in."

Selection Vs. Screening Interviews

The process to which the majority of this chapter is devoted is the actual *selection interview*, usually conducted by the person to whom the new hire will be reporting. But there is another process—the *screening interview*—which many of you may have to survive first.

Screening interviews are usually conducted by a member of the personnel department. Though they may not be empowered to hire, they *are* in a position to screen out or eliminate those candidates they feel (based on the facts) are not qualified to handle the job. These decisions are not usually made on the basis of personality, appearance, eloquence, persuasiveness or any other subjective criteria, but rather by clicking off yes or no answers against a checklist of skills. If you don't have the requisite number, you will be eliminated from further consideration. This may seem arbitrary, but it is a realistic and often necessary way for corporations to minimize the time and dollars involved in filling even the lowest jobs on the corporate ladder.

Remember, screening personnel are not looking for reasons to *hire* you; they're trying to find ways to *eliminate* you from the job search pack. Resumes sent blindly to the personnel department will usually be subjected to such screening; you will be eliminated without any personal contact (an excellent reason to construct a superior resume and *not* send out blind mailings).

If you are contacted, it will most likely be by telephone. When you are responding to such a call, keep these three things in mind: 1). It *is* an interview; be on your guard. 2). Answer all questions honestly. And 3). Be enthusiastic. You will get the standard questions from the interviewer— his or her attempts to "flesh out" the information included on your resume and/or cover letter. Strictly speaking, they are seeking out any negatives which may exist. If your resume is honest and factual (and it should be), you have no reason to be anxious, because you have nothing to hide.

Don't be nervous—be glad you were called and remember your objective: to get past this screening phase so you can get on to the real interview.

The Day Of The Interview

On the day of the interview, wear a conservative (not funereal) business suit—*not* a sports coat, *not* a "nice" blouse and skirt. Shoes should be shined, nails cleaned, hair cut and in place. And no low-cut or tight-fitting dresses (especially on the men).

It's not unusual for resumes and cover letters to head in different directions when a company starts passing them around to a number of executives. If you sent them, both may even be long gone. So bring along extra copies of your resume and your own copy of the cover letter that originally accompanied it.

Whether or not you make them available, we suggest you prepare a neatly-typed list of references (including the name, title, company, address and phone number of each person). You may want to bring along a copy of your high school or college transcript, especially if it's something to brag about. (Once you get your first job, you'll probably never use it—or be asked for it—again, so enjoy it while you can!)

On Time Means Fifteen Minutes Early

Plan to arrive fifteen minutes before your scheduled appointment. If you're in an unfamiliar city or have a long drive to their offices, allow extra time for the unexpected delays that seem to occur with mind-numbing regularity on important days.

Arriving early will give you some time to check your appearance, catch your breath, check in with the receptionist, learn how to correctly pronounce the interviewer's name, and get yourself organized and battle ready.

Arriving late does not make a sterling first impression. If you are only a few minutes late, it's probably best not to mention it or even excuse yourself. With a little luck, everybody else is behind schedule and no one will notice. However, if you're more than fifteen minutes late, have an honest (or at least *serviceable*) explanation ready and offer it at your first opportunity. Then drop the subject as quickly as possible and move on to the interview.

The Eyes Have It

When you meet the interviewer, shake hands firmly. People notice handshakes and often form a first impression based solely on them.

Ask for a business card. This will make sure you get the person's name and title right when you write your follow-up letter. You can staple it to the company file for easy reference as you continue your networking.

Try to maintain eye contact with the interviewer as you talk. This will indicate you're interested in what he or she has to say. Sit straight. Avoid smoking.

Should coffee or a soft drink be offered, you may accept (but should do so only if the interviewer is joining you).

Keep your voice at a comfortable level, and try to sound enthusiastic (without imitating Charleen Cheerleader). Be confident and poised, and provide direct, accurate and honest answers to the trickiest questions.

And, as you try to remember all this, just be yourself, and try to act like you're comfortable and almost enjoying this whole process!

Don't Name Drop...Conspicuously

A friendly relationship with other company employees may have provided you with valuable information prior to the interview, but don't flaunt such relationships. The interviewer is interested only in how you will relate to him or her and how well he or she surmises you will fit in with the rest of the staff. Name dropping may smack of favoritism. And you are in no position to know who the interviewer's favorite (or *least* favorite) people are.

On the other hand, if you have established a complex network of professionals through informational interviews, attending trade shows, reading trade magazines, etc., it is perfectly permissable to refer to these people, their companies, conversations you've had, whatever. It may even impress the interviewer with the extensiveness of your preparation.

Fork On The Left, Knife On The Right

Interviews are sometimes conducted over lunch, though this is not usually the case with entry-level people. If it does happen to you, though, try to order something in the middle price range, neither filet mignon nor a cheeseburger.

Do not order alcohol. If your interviewer orders a carafe of wine, you may share it. Otherwise, alcohol should be considered *verboten*, under any and all circumstances. Then hope your mother taught you the correct way to eat and talk at the same time. If not, just do your best to maintain your poise.

The Importance Of *Last* Impressions

There are some things interviewers will always view with displeasure: street language, complete lack of eye contact, insufficient or vague explanations or answers, a noticeable lack of energy, poor interpersonal skills (i.e., not listening or the basic inability to carry on an intelligent conversation), and a demonstrable lack of motivation.

Every impression may count. And the very *last* impression an interviewer has may outweigh everything else. So, before you allow an interview to end, summarize why you want the job, why you are qualified, and what, *in particular*, you can offer their company.

Then, take some action. If the interviewer hasn't told you about the rest of the interview process and/or where you stand, ask him or her. Will you be seeing other people that day? If so, ask for some background on anyone else with whom you'll be interviewing. If there are no other meetings that day, what's the next step? When can you expect to hear from them about coming back?

When you return home, file all the business cards, copies of correspondence and notes from the interview(s) with each company in the appropriate files. Finally, but most importantly, ask yourself which firms you really want to work for and which you are no longer interested in. This will quickly determine how far you want the process at each to develop before you politely tell them to stop considering you for the job.

Immediately send a thank-you letter to each executive you met. These should, of course, be neatly-typed business letters, not handwritten notes (unless you are most friendly, indeed, with the interviewer and want to *stress* the "informal" nature of your note). If you are still interested in pursuing a position at their company, tell them in no uncertain terms. Reiterate why you feel you're the best candidate and tell each of the executives when you hope (expect?) to hear from them.

On The 8th Day God Created Interviewers

Though most interviews will follow a relatively standard format, there will undoubtedly be a wide disparity in the skills of the interviewers you meet. Many of these executives (with the exception of the Personnel staff) will most likely not have extensive interviewing experience, have limited knowledge of interviewing techniques, use them infrequently, be hurried or harried by the press of other duties or not even view your interview as critically important.

Rather than studying standardized test results or utilizing professional evaluation skills developed over many years of practice, these non-professionals react intuitively—their initial (first five minutes) impressions are often the lasting and overriding factors they remember. So you must sell yourself ...fast.

The best way to do this is to try to achieve a comfort level with your interviewer. Isn't establishing rapport—through words, gestures, appearance common interests, etc. —what you try to do in *any* social situation? It's just trying to know one another better. Against this backdrop, the questions and answers will flow in a more natural way.

The Set Sequence

Irrespective of the competence levels of the interviewer, you can anticipate an interview sequence roughly as follows:

- Greetings
- Social niceties (small talk)
- Purpose of meeting (let's get down to business)
- Broad questions/answers
- Specific questions/answers
- In-depth discussion of company, job and opportunity
- Summarizing information given & received
- Possible salary probe (dependent upon level of achievement)
- Summary/indication as to next steps

When you look at this sequence closely, it is obvious that once you have gotten past the greeting, social niceties and some explanation of the job (in the "getting down to business" section), the bulk of the interview will be questions—yours and the interviewer's. In this question and answer session, there are not necessarily any right or wrong answers, only good and bad ones.

It's Time To Play Q & A

You can't control the "chemistry" between you and the interviewer—do you seem to "hit it off" right from the start or never connect at all? Since you *can't* control such a subjective problem, it pays to focus on what you *can* —the questions you will be asked, your answers and the questions *you* had better be prepared to ask.

Not surprisingly, many of the same questions pop up in interview after interview, regardless of company size, type or location. I have chosen the thirteen most common—along with appropriate hints and answers for each—for inclusion in this chapter. Remember: There are no right or wrong answers to these questions, only good and bad ones.

Substance counts more than speed when answering questions. Take your time and make sure that you listen to each question—there is nothing quite as disquieting as a lengthy, well-thoughtout answer that is completely irrelevant to the question asked. You wind up looking like a programmed clone with stock answers to dozens of questions who has, unfortunately, pulled the wrong one out of the grab bag.

Once you have adequately answered a specific question, it *is* permissible to go beyond it and add more information if doing so adds something to the discussion and/or highlights a particular strength, skill, course, etc. But avoid making lengthy speeches just for the sake of sounding off.

Study the list of questions (and hints) that follow, and prepare at least one solid, concise answer for each. Practice with a friend until your answers to these most-asked questions sound intelligent, professional and, most important, unmemorized and unrehearsed.

"Why do you want to be in this field?"

Using your knowledge and understanding of the particular field, explain why you find the business exciting and where and how you see yourself fitting in.

"Why do you think you will be successful in this business?"

Using the information from your self evaluation and the research you did on that particular company, formulate an answer which marries your strengths to theirs and to the characteristics of the position for which you're applying.

"Why did you choose our company?"

This is an excellent opportunity to explain the extensive process of education and research you've undertaken. Tell them about your strengths and how you match up with their firm. Emphasize specific things about their company that led you to seek an interview. Be a salesperson—be convincing.

"What can you do for us?"

Construct an answer that essentially lists your strengths, the experience you have which will contribute to your job performance, and any other unique qualifications that will place you at the head of the applicant pack. Be careful: This is a question specifically designed to *eliminate* some of that pack. Sell yourself. Be one of the few called back for a second interview.

"What position here interests you?"

If you're interviewing for a specific position, answer accordingly. If you want to make sure you don't close the door on other opportunities of which you might be unaware, you can follow up with your own question: "I'm here to apply for your Sales Training Program. Is there another position open for which you feel I'm qualified?"

If you've arranged an interview with a company without knowing of any specific openings, use the answer to this question to describe the kind of work you'd like to do and why you're qualified to do it. Avoid a specific job title, since they will tend to vary from firm to firm.

If you're on a first interview with the personnel department, just answer the question. They only want to figure out where to send you.

"What jobs have you held and why did you leave them?"

Or the direct approach: "Have you ever been fired?" Take this opportunity to expand on your resume, rather than precisely answering the question by merely recapping your job experiences. In discussing each job, point out what you liked about it, what factors led to your leaving and how the next job added to your continuing professional education. If you *have* been fired, say so. It's very easy to check.

"What are your strengths and weaknesses?"

Or "**What are your hobbies (or outside interests)?**" Both questions can be easily answered using the data you gathered to complete the self-evaluation process. Be wary of being too forthcoming about your glaring faults (nobody expects you to volunteer every weakness and mistake), but do *not* reply, "I don't have any." They won't believe you and, what's worse, *you* won't believe you. After all, you did the evaluation—you know it's a lie!

Good answers to these questions are those in which the interviewer can identify benefits for him- or herself. For example: "I consider myself an excellent planner. I am seldom caught by surprise and I pride myself on being able to anticipate problems and schedule my time to be ahead of the game. I devote a prescribed number of hours each week to this activity. I've noticed that many people just react. If you plan ahead, you should be able to cut off most problems before they arise."

You may consider disarming the interviewer by admitting a weakness, but doing it in such a way as to make it relatively unimportant to the job function. For example: "Higher mathematics has never been my strong suit. Though I am competent enough, I've always envied my friends with a more mathematical bent. In sales, though, I haven't found this a liability. I'm certainly quick enough in figuring out how close I am to monthly quotas and, of course, I keep a running record of commissions earned."

"Do you think your extracurricular activities were worth the time you devoted to them?"

This is a question often asked of entry-level candidates. One possible answer: "Very definitely. As you see from my resume, I have been quite active in the Student Government and

French Club. My language fluency allowed me to spend my junior year abroad as an exchange student, and working in a functioning government gave me firsthand knowledge of what can be accomplished with people in the real world. I suspect my marks would have been somewhat higher had I not taken on so many activities outside of school, but I feel the balance they gave me contributed significantly to my overall growth as a person."

"What are your career goals?"

Interviewers are always seeking to probe the motivations of prospective employees. Nowhere is this more apparent than when the area of ambition is discussed. The high key answer to this question might be; "Given hard work, company growth and a few lucky breaks along the way, I'd look forward to being in a top executive position by the time I'm 35. I believe in effort and the risk/reward system—my research on this company has shown me that it operates on the same principles. I would hope it would select its future leaders from those people who displaying such characteristics."

"At some future date would you be willing to relocate?"

Pulling up one's roots is not the easiest thing in the world to do, but it is often a fact of life in the corporate world. If you're serious about your career (and such a move often represents a step up the career ladder), you will probably not mind such a move. Tell the interviewer. If you really *don't* want to move, you may want to say so, too—though I would find out how probable or frequent such relocations would be before closing the door while still in the interview stage.

Keep in mind that as you get older, establish ties in a particular community, marry, have children, etc., you will inevitably feel less jubilation at the thought of moving once a year or even "being out on the road." So take the opportunity to experience new places and experiences while you're young. If you don't, you may never get the chance.

"How did you get along with your last supervisor?"

This question is designed to understand your relationship with (and reaction to) authority. Remember: Companies look for team players, people who will fit in with their hierarchy, their rules, their ways of doing things. An answer might be: "I prefer to work with smart, strong people who know what they want and can express themselves. I learned in the military that in order to accomplish the mission, someone has to be the leader and that person has to be given the authority to lead. Someday I aim to be that leader. I hope then my subordinates will follow me as much and as competently as I'm ready to follow now."

"What are your salary requirements?"

If they are at all interested in you, this question will probably come up. The danger is that you may price yourself too low or, even worse, right out of a job you want. Since you will have a general idea of industry figures for that position (and may even have an idea of what that company tends to pay new people for the position), why not refer to a *range* of salaries, such as $20,000 - $25,000?

If the interviewer doesn't bring up salary at all, it's doubtful you're being seriously considered, so you probably don't need to even bring the subject up. (If you know you aren't getting the job or aren't interested in it if offered, you may try to nail down a salary figure in order to be better prepared for the next interview.)

"Tell me about yourself"

Watch out for this one! It's often one of the first questions asked. If you falter here, the rest of the interview could quickly become a downward slide to nowhere. Be prepared, and consider it an opportunity to combine your answers to many of the previous questions into one concise description of who you are, what you want to be and why that company should take a chance on you. Summarize your resume—briefly—and expand on particular courses or experiences relevant to the firm or position. Do *not* go on about your hobbies or personal life, where you spent your summer vacation, or anything that is not relevant to securing that job. You may explain how that particular job fits in with your long-range career goals and talk specifically about what attracted you to their company in the first place.

The Not-So-Obvious Questions

Every interviewer is different and, unfortunately, there are no rules saying he or she has to use all or any of the "basic" questions covered above. But we think the odds are against his or her avoiding *all* of them. Whichever of these he or she includes, be assured most interviewers do like to come up with questions that are "uniquely theirs." It may be just one or a whole series—questions developed over the years that he or she feels help separate the wheat from the chaff.

You can't exactly prepare yourself for questions like, "What would you do if...(fill in the blank with some obscure occurrence)?" "Tell me about your father," or "What's your favorite ice cream flavor?" Every interviewer we know has his or her favorites and all of these questions seem to come out of left field. Just stay relaxed, grit your teeth (quietly) and take a few seconds to frame a reasonably intelligent reply.

Some questions may be downright inappropriate. Young women, for example, may be asked about their plans for marriage and children. Don't call the interviewer a chauvinist (or worse). And don't point out that the question may be a little outside the law—the nonprofessional interviewer may not realize such questions are illegal, and a huffy response may confuse, even anger, him or her.

Whenever any questions are raised about your personal life—and this question surely qualifies—it is much more effective to respond that you are very interested in the position and have no reason to believe that your personal life will preclude you from doing an excellent job.

"Do You Have Any Questions?"

It's the last fatal question on our list, often the last one an interviewer throws at you after an hour or two of grilling. Unless the interview has been very long and unusually thorough, you probably *should* have questions—about the job, the company, even the industry. Unfortunately, by the time this question off-handedly hits the floor, you are already looking forward to leaving and may have absolutely nothing to say.

Preparing yourself for an interview means more than having answers for some of the questions an interviewer may ask. It means having your *own* set of questions—at least five or six—for the interviewer. The interviewer is trying to find the right person for the job. *You're* trying to find the right job. So you should be just as curious about him or her and the company as he or she is about you. Here's a short list of questions you may consider asking on any interview:

1. What will my typical day be like?
2. What happened to the last person who had this job?
3. Why did you come to work here? What keeps you here?

4. Given my attitude and qualifications, how would you estimate my chances for career advancement at your company?

5. If you were I, would you start here again?

6. How would you characterize the management philosophy of your firm?

7. What characteristics do the successful_____ at your company have in common (fill in the blank with an appropriate title)?

8. What's the best (and worst) thing about working here?

9. On a scale of 1 to 10, how would you rate your company—in terms of salaries, benefits and employee satisfaction—in comparison to similar firms?

Testing & Applications

Though not part of the selection interview itself, job applications and psychological testing are often part of the pre-interview process. You should know something about them.

The job application is essentially a record-keeping exercise—simply the transfer of work experience and educational data from your resume to a printed applications form. Though taking the time to recopy data may seem like a waste of time, some companies simply want the information in a particular order on a standard form. One difference: Applications often require the listing of references and salary levels achieved. Be sure to bring your list of references with you to any interview (so you can transfer the pertinent information), and don't lie about salary history; it's easily checked.

Many companies now use a variety of psychological tests as additional mechanisms to screen out undesirable candidates. Although their accuracy is subject to question, the companies that use them obviously believe they are effective at identifying applicants whose personality makeups would preclude their participating positively in a given work situation, especially those at the extreme ends of the behavior spectrum.

Their usefulness in predicting job accomplishment is considered limited. If you are normal (like the rest of us), you'll have no trouble with these tests and may even find them amusing. Just don't try to outsmart them—you'll just wind up outsmarting yourself.

Section 3

Job Opportunities Databank

21

U.S. And Canadian
Entry-Level Job Listings

Now that you have read through the articles by top professionals on possible careers available to you in radio and television, where can you find a station or company that will give you your first job in the particular area you've chosen?

While there are numerous corporate directories and other reference works (many of them cited in our job search section) that contain important background information on companies in which you may be interested, none of them can help you identify those that are actively seeking and hiring entry-level people.

This chapter does exactly that, giving you the detailed information you need on the biggest and most important radio and television stations and networks in both the U. S. and Canada. The detailed data included here is not a compendium of information from other sources. *We have printed only the information we obtained directly from the stations or companies themselves.* This information was compiled by our staff through direct mail questionnaires and telephone calls and represents data that is completely unavailable anywhere else.

As should be obvious, this is not a *complete* listing of U. S. and Canadian stations. It is not meant to be. But if studied and used properly, it should help you identify those stations that offer the best entry-level opportunities. Note that we have tended to list group ownership companies (or headquarters)—which may own hundreds of stations—rather than individually list each of those stations. Contact those companies directly for more information on each of their stations.

With the group ownership listings as a guide, you should be able to get a better feel for the possibilities out there. By referring to the *Broadcasting Cable Yearbook,* you will find a complete listing of individual stations under each group ownership. You can then use the reference works cited elsewhere in this *Career Directory* to find other stations that match those listed here in size or location.

Most of the information should be self-explanatory.

"Average Entry-level Hiring" is that station's best estimate of anticipated need for new people each year. *"Total employees"* lists all full-time employees. Part-time employees, if any, are noted in parentheses.

Two important points: 1) A "?" following the "average entry-level hiring" entry means *they tend to hire entry-level people;* **they were just unable to come up with any specific number. 2) If the station indicates they do not plan to hire any entry-level people, they may still have listed "Opportunities." In this case, these should not be considered actual jobs, merely the positions they consider entry-level...whether or not they currently have openings.**

If the stations themselves had any specific suggestions, we've included them. These will help you get a head start on other applicants—you'll know what they want you to do!

The *"Internships"* listing ("yes" or "no") is to let you know whether that company and/or its member stations have internship programs for students. You will notice that the vast majority of stations in this listing responded "yes"—and that many of them stressed the important of an internship for an entry-level person.

Since internship programs are viewed so highly, we have included detailed internship information from all these stations and companies in our newly published *Internships: Volume 5, Radio & Television, Broadcasting & Production.*

One final note: Despite our every attempt to ensure the accuracy of the information we've included, time marches on...and so do contacts. In other words, there will be mistakes in these listings—the very day they're published—just because things change and, in some stations, change very quickly. But we think you'll find that the vast majority of this previously-unpublished information will remain credible until it is updated in 1993 in a second edition.

Nevertheless, if you've narrowed your target list down to a manageable number of stations, we suggest you double-check the contact name before mailing out your (no doubt brilliantly written) resume and cover letter.

Good luck!

ABILENE RADIO & TV STATIONS
4510 South 14th Street
Abilene, TX 79605
915-692-4242
Employment Contact: Joyce Proffitt,
Accounting Manager
Total Employees: 65-70
Average Entry-Level Hiring: As needed.
Internships: Yes

ACKERLEY COMMUNICATIONS INC.
800 Fifth Avenue—Suite 3770
Seattle, WA 98104
206-624-2888
Employment Contact: Joanie, Director of
Communications
Total Employees: ?
Average Entry-Level Hiring: ?
Opportunities: Stations hire indepen-
dently. Need college degree and work
experience; not many entry-level posi-
tions available.
Comments: "Must have perseverance and
know what you want to do."
Internships: Yes

**ALLEGHENY MOUNTAIN NETWORK
STATIONS**
Box 204, State College, PA 16804
814-238-0792
Employment Contact: Matt Swayne
Total Employees: 40
Average Entry-Level Hiring: 3-4
Opportunities: Sales—Four year college
degree; work part-time at college station
while in school. Broadcasting—H.S. edu-
cation; work as entry-level disc jockey.
Comments: "If you hope to work on the
air, we look for a good voice and
motivation."
Internships: Yes

**AMERICAN FAMILY BROADCAST
GROUP INC.**
1932 Wynnton Road
Columbus, GA 31999
404-596-5853
Employment Contact: Brenda Owens,
Recruiter

Total Employees: 15 at this office; 1,200 in
corporation
Average Entry-Level Hiring: 30
Opportunities: Secretary, Clerical—High
school education, typing and correspondence skills.
Comments: "We look for a neat appearance and an outstanding personality."
Internships: No

AMERICAN MEDIA INC.
66 Colonial Drive
Patchogue, NY 11772
516-475-5200
Employment Contact: Ellen Beck
Total Employees: 40
Average Entry-Level Hiring: 2-3
Opportunities: Sales, Traffic—No
requirement on education; prior exper-
ience helpful and good presentation.
Accounting—Degree required.
Comments: "For Broadcasting and Sales,
we look for self-motivation and a good
personality."
Internships: Yes

**ANDREWS-CLANCY-MANCE
COMMUNICATIONS**
199 Wealtha Avenue
Watertown, NY 13601
315-782-1240
Employment Contact: Karen Strite
Total Employees: 15
Average Entry-Level Hiring: 3
Opportunities: On-Air, Production—
College degree required.
Comments: "We look for energetic people
with initiative."
Internships: Yes

ANNAPOLIS VALLEY RADIO LTD.
29 Oakdene Street—Box 310
Kentville, NS B4N 1H5
902-678-2111
Employment Contact: Diane Best-
Redden—Head of Human Resources
Total Employees: 50
Average Entry-Level Hiring: 3

Opportunities: Broadcasting—Secondary education with radio and TV courses required; college degree preferred.
Comments: "We look for bright, motivated and flexible people."
Internships: Yes

AP NETWORK NEWS
50 Rockefeller Plaza
New York, NY 10020
212-621-1500
Employment Contact: Human Resources
Total Employees: 800 in NY; 3,000 worldwide
Average Entry-Level Hiring: 50
Opportunities: Editorial—At least 18 months experience on a daily newspaper required; anything less than that qualifies you for a temporary position. Secretarial—Knowledge of Word Perfect 5.1 and secretarial skills required; knowledge of Lotus a plus.
Comments: "Send resume and cover letter to Human Resources. If you are interested in journalism or editorial, please send a couple of pieces."
Internships: Yes

ARMADALE COMMUNICATIONS LTD.
Toronto-Buttonville Airport
Markham, ON L3P 3J9
416-477-8000
Employment Contact: Liz Osborne, Personnel & Payroll
Total Employees: ? (6 Canadian stations)
Average Entry-Level Hiring: Depends on openings.
Opportunities: Publishing—Work on school newspaper or community theatre. Placement Service for Training—Commitment to working while in college. High school co-op program—Apply to work a couple of months out of the year to work in the station.
Comments: "Voice and personality are very important; capabilities, uniqueness and initiative are welcomed."
Internships: ?

ASTOR BROADCAST GROUP
1623 Fifth Avenue
San Rafael, CA 94901
415-456-1510
Employment Contact: Rebecca Ward, Traffic Manager
Total Employees: 20
Average Entry-Level Hiring: Varies
Opportunities: Advertising—College degree preferred. Broadcasting—No experience necessary.
Comments: "Must love the job since the salaries can be low in the beginning."
Internships: Yes

ATLANTIC VENTURES CORP.
40 Beach Street—Suite 200
Manchester, MA 01944
508-526-8132
Employment Contact: Kathy Haley, Corporate Office
Total Employees: 200
Average Entry-Level Hiring: 1
Opportunities: On-Air—College degree required. Sales—College degree required; prior experience helpful.
Internships: Yes

BAHAKEL COMMUNICATIONS
3020 Eastern Boulevard
Montgomery, AL 36116
205-279-8787
Employment Contact: John Rogers, General Manager
Total Employees: 18 (News)
Average Entry-Level Hiring: 2-3
Opportunities: News—Degree in journalism preferred.
Comments: "Looking for motivated people."
Internships: Yes

BATON BROADCASTING INC.
9 Channel Nine Court
Toronto, ON M1S 4B5
416-299-2000
Employment Contact: George Platkin, Employment Manager
Total Employees: ?

Average Entry-Level Hiring: ?
Opportunities: College graduates in journalism, radio and TV welcome.
Internships: No

BEACH-SCHMIDT GROUP
Box 817
Hays, KS 67601
913-625-2578

Employment Contact: Janet Hays, Business Manager
Total Employees: 40-50
Average Entry-Level Hiring: 3-4
Opportunities: Broadcasting—College degree in journalism or broadcasting. Sales—Experience required; good aptitude for selling.
Internships: Yes

BECK-ROSS COMMUNICATIONS INC.
3090 Route 112
Medford, NY 11763
516-732-1061

Employment Contact: Jessica Surbeck, Station Manager
Total Employees: 35-40
Average Entry-Level Hiring: Varies.
Opportunities: On-Air—College degree required. All other positions—Should be well educated and have experience at college stations.
Internships: Yes

BIBLE BROADCASTING NETWORK
Box 1818
Chesapeake, VA 23327
804-547-9421

Employment Contact: Leo Galletta, Network Operations Manager
Total Employees: 25 at headquarters, 65 in network
Average Entry-Level Hiring: 4-5
Opportunities: Announcer, Manager Trainee—Bachelor's degree (preferably from a seminary or Christian college, but not required). No experience necessary, will train.

Comments: "Must feel at ease before the public and be willing to relocate when new stations are built."
Internships: No

BIG HORN COMMUNICATIONS INC.
P.O. Box 23309
Billings, MT 59104
406-652-4743

Employment Contact: Pat Rookhuizen, Receptionist
Total Employees: 25
Average Entry-Level Hiring: 5
Opportunities: Sales—College degree not required.
Comments: "Must have common sense and nice appearance."
Internships: No

BILBAT RADIO INC.
Box 726
Hornell, NY 14843
607-324-2000

Employment Contact: Lynn O'Brian, Program Director
Total Employees: 18
Average Entry-Level Hiring: 5-10
Opportunities: Any position—Experience helpful but will train. Looking for new talent and good personalities.
Comments: "Must be flexible and motivated."
Internships: No

BINGHAM COMMUNICATIONS GROUP
1200 Westlake Avenue North—Suite 707
Seattle, WA 98109
206-285-8500

Employment Contact: Barbara Buchanan, Accounting Office
Total Employees: 50 total, 4 in corporate office
Average Entry-Level Hiring: 10-20
Opportunities: On-Air—Broadcasting experience helpful. Sales, Account Executive, Office Positions—Skill requirements depend on positions.

Comments: "Corporate headquarters does not do the hiring, but we will send you applications for the stations. Call for information."
Internships: Yes

BLADE COMMUNICATIONS INC.
541 Superior Street
Toledo, OH 43660
419-245-6206

Employment Contact: Bernice Urbina, Manager of Employee Development
Total Employees: ?
Average Entry-Level Hiring: 0
Opportunities: Minimum of 2-3 years experience with a college degree for all positions.
Comments: "It is important to get experience while in school."
Internships: Yes

BLOOMINGTON BROADCASTING CO. INC.
Box 8
Bloomington, IL 61702
309-829-1221

Employment Contact: Carole Rodgers, Controller
Total Employees: 5 full-time, 20 part-time
Average Entry-Level Hiring: 1
Opportunities: Announcing—College degree preferred. News—College degree required.
Comments: "Looking for people with a good voice and personality."
Internships: Yes

BONNEVILLE INTERNATIONAL CORP.
Broadcast House—Box 1160
Salt Lake City, UT 84110
801-575-7510

Employment Contact: Joan Bishop, VP of Employee Relations
Total Employees: 1,400
Average Entry-Level Hiring: ?
Opportunities: College degree or equivalent required; experience helpful.

Comments: "Call and we will send you an application; these are kept on file for one year."
Internships: Yes

BOOTH AMERICAN CO.
645 Griswold—Suite 633
Detroit, MI 48226
313-965-2000

Employment Contact: Steve Hegwood, Program/Director of Operations
Total Employees: 50
Average Entry-Level Hiring: ?
Opportunities: News—College degree required; 2-3 years of professional experience preferred.
Internships: Yes

BORGEN BROADCASTING CO.
Box 377
Preston, MN 55965
507-765-3856

Employment Contact: Janna Vaalemoen, Controller
Total Employees: ?
Average Entry-Level Hiring: ?
Opportunities: Announcers—Broadcasting experience preferred but will train. Copy Department—Writing and creative abilities.
Internships: No

BOTT BROADCASTING COMPANY
10550 Barley
Overland Park, KS 66212
913-642-7600

Employment Contact: Bill Pelletier, Announcer; Ken Monroe, Program Director
Total Employees: 5 full-time, 4-5 part-time
Average Entry-Level Hiring: 1-2
Opportunities: Part-time weekend positions (titles not specified)—While working in high school or just out of college. Board Operators—Duties and requirements not specified.
Internships: No

BREWER BROADCASTING CORP.
Box 397
Tell City, IN 47586
812-547-2345

Employment Contact: Brenda Bryant, Personnel
Total Employees: ?
Average Entry-Level Hiring: 2-3
Opportunities: Broadcasting, Sales—Will train.
Comments: "Looking for reliable people with a good personality."
Internships: No

BRITISH COLUMBIA TELEVISION BROADCASTING SYSTEM LTD.
Box 4700
Vancouver, BC V6B 4A3
604-420-2288

Employment Contact: Sandra Hamm, Personnel
Total Employees: 350
Average Entry-Level Hiring: 2
Opportunities: Technical—Two year college preferred. News, Production—Two year college minimum; 2-3 years experience at a smaller station.
Comments: "Must have a great interest in current affairs."
Internships: No

BUCKLEY BROADCASTING CORP.
166 West Putnam Avenue
Greenwich, CT 06830
203-661-4307

Employment Contact: Tom Nantzarides
Total Employees: ?
Average Entry-Level Hiring: ?
Opportunities: Broadcasting—Degree preferred; work experience at college station helpful. Sales—Experience required.
Comments: "Try to get work at local stations first if you would really like to be on the air."
Internships: ?

BURBACH BROADCASTING GROUP
2510 One PPG Place, Pittsburgh, PA 15222
814-237-4959

Employment Contact: Dave Burdette, General Manager
Total Employees: ?
Average Entry-Level Hiring: 7-8
Opportunities: News—College degree required. Broadcasting—will hire part-time announcers without degrees; good voice quality helpful.
Internships: Yes

BUSSE BROADCASTING CORP.
590 West Maple Street
Kalamazoo, MI 49008
616-388-8019
Employment Contact: David Comisar, VP Broadcasting Service
Total Employees: 108
Average Entry-Level Hiring: 7-8
Opportunities: Production, Studio, Generator Operators—Degree in communications or broadcasting helpful; will train.
Internships: Yes

CALIFORNIA BROADCASTING
P.O. Box 81380, Salinas, CA 93912
408-422-7484

Employment Contact: Pat Toeliver, Human Resources/Business Manager
Total Employees: ?
Average Entry-Level Hiring: ?
Opportunities: Sales—College degree required; sales oriented. Broadcasting—Experience necessary. Traffic—Some college helpful, will train.
Comments: "Motivation is a plus."
Internships: Yes

CALIFORNIA OREGON BROADCASTING INC.
Box 5M
Medford, OR 97501
503-779-5555
Employment Contact: Becky Barry, Staff Accountant

Total Employees: 200
Average Entry-Level Hiring: ?
Opportunities: News—No requirements specified.
Internships: Yes

THE CANXUS BROADCASTING CORP.
Box 937
Caribou, ME 04736
207-473-7513

Employment Contact: Pam Curley, Traffic Manager
Total Employees: 12 full-time, 4 part-time
Average Entry-Level Hiring: 1-2
Opportunities: News—College degree is an asset; journalism major preferred, communications degree not necessary.
Comments: "Must like to read, have a good voice and personality."
Internships: No

CAPITAL CITIES
(American Broadcasting Corp.—ABC)
77 West 66th Street
New York, NY 10022
212-456-7777

Employment Contact: Margaret Agosta, Information Coordinator
Total Employees: 2,000
Average Entry-Level Hiring: ?
Opportunities: Clerical, Secretary, Research Clerk—College degree preferred but not required.
Comments: "Must be a team player."
Internships: Yes

CAPITOL BROADCASTING CO. INC.
Box 12000
Raleigh, NC 27605
919-890-6000

Employment Contact: Ron Price, Corporate Director
Total Employees: 600
Average Entry-Level Hiring: 4-5
Opportunities: News, Production—College degree and 3 or 4 years experience in a smaller station.

Comments: "We require a high degree of commitment to quality."
Internships: No

CAROLINA CHRISTIAN BROADCASTING INC.
Box 1616
Greenville, SC 29602
803-244-1616

Employment Contact: Norma Barnett, Office Manager
Total Employees: 50
Average Entry-Level Hiring: 3
Opportunities: Production, Programming—Degree required. Production people should have technical training.
Internships: Yes

CBS INC.
51 West 52nd Street
New York, NY 10019
212-975-4321

Employment Contact: Personnel
Total Employees: 6,500 and downsizing
Average Entry-Level Hiring: 0-100
Opportunities: Administrative Assistant, Support Staff in various areas—College degree, office skills, and 50 WPM typing required.
Internships: Yes

CD BROADCASTING CORP.
5200 Wilson Road, No. 308
Minneapolis, MN 55424
612-924-0502

Employment Contact: Charlie Fergneson, General Manager
Total Employees: ?
Average Entry-Level Hiring: 2
Opportunities: Marketing—College degree or experience.
Comments: "Must be able to express yourself verbally and have good writing skills."
Internships: Yes

CENTURY BROADCASTING CORP.
875 North Michigan Avenue
Suite 1510
Chicago, IL 60611
312-440-3100

Employment Contact: Hope Daniels, Director of Public Affairs
Total Employees: ?
Average Entry-Level Hiring: ?
Opportunities: Any position requires experience.
Comments: "We consider internship experience very important."
Internships: Yes

CHRISTIAN FAITH BROADCASTING INC.
3809 Maple Avenue
Castalia, OH 44824
419-684-5311

Employment Contact: Marie White, Secretary
Total Employees: 23
Average Entry-Level Hiring: 2-4
Opportunities: Positions do not require background or experience; we will train.
Comments: "We look for people interested in ministry."
Internships: Yes

CLEAR CHANNEL COMMUNICATIONS INC.
P.O. Box 659512
San Antonio, TX 78265
512-822-2828

Employment Contact: Valerie Fisher, Payroll/Benefits
Total Employees: ?
Average Entry-Level Hiring: ?
Opportunities: Sales, Broadcasting, Accounting—College major. No other requirements specified.
Comments: "Looking for outgoing, eager people who will work hard for the company."
Internships: Yes

COMMUNITY & BURNS BROADCASTING
Box 1176
Los Alamos, NM 87544
505-662-4342

Employment Contact: Tony Fitch, Programmer/Director
Total Employees: 8
Average Entry-Level Hiring: 1
Opportunities: News—College degree helpful; internship during high school years a plus. Broadcasting—Writing skills required, college degree not necessary.
Comments: "Looking for smart and enthusiastic people."
Internships: Yes

COSMOS BROADCASTING CORP.
P.O. Box 39270
Louisville, KY 40232
502-585-2201

Employment Contact: Nancy Smith, Executive Secretary
Total Employees: 10 at corporate office, 610 total
Average Entry-Level Hiring: ?
Opportunities: Production Operator—Previous experience at TV station required.
Comments: "Experience is always required—look into getting it in an internship."
Internships: Yes

CR BROADCASTING
344 Old Pinson Road
Jackson, TN 38301
901-424-1200

Employment Contact: Sherry, Personnel
Total Employees: ?
Average Entry-Level Hiring: 10
Opportunities: On-Air, Sales—College degree is beneficial. No other requirements specified.
Internships: No

CRB BROADCASTING
630 Fifth Avenue
New York, NY 10111
212-581-7550

Employment Contact: Julia Klise
Total Employees: ?
Average Entry-Level Hiring: 2
Opportunities: All positions require a college degree. No other information obtained.
Comments: "Looking for enthusiastic, motivated people with a great personality."
Internships: No

THE CROMWELL GROUP INC.
Box 150846
Nashville, TN 37215
615-383-7560

Employment Contact: Ken Athon, Controller
Total Employees: 30-40
Average Entry-Level Hiring: 4-5
Opportunities: News—College degree preferred; good English and writing skills. Sales—Experience preferred; courses at Carnegie helpful.
Internships: No

CROSSROAD RADIO INC.
Box 1590
Swainsboro, GA 30401
912-237-1590

Employment Contact: Roy Thompson, Owner/General Manager
Total Employees: 6
Average Entry-Level Hiring: 2
Opportunities: Any position—Experience preferred. No other requirements specified.
Internships: No

DAVIS BROADCASTING INC.
1115 14th Street
Columbus, GA 31903
404-576-3565

Employment Contact: Arthur Thomason
Total Employees: 45

Average Entry-Level Hiring: ?
Opportunities: Sales—College classes in marketing. On-Air—College preferred.
Comments: "Articulation and a pleasant voice are a plus."
Internships: Yes

DAVIS-GOLDFARB CO.
2121 Ave. of the Stars—Suite 2800
Los Angeles, CA 90067
213-551-2288

Employment Contact: Joseph Goldfarb, Manager
Total Employees: 50-60
Average Entry-Level Hiring: 2-3
Opportunities: News—College graduate; journalism majors with writing skills.
Comments: "We encourage people to get an internship."
Internships: Yes

DEMAREE MEDIA INC.
1780 Holly Street—Box 878
Fayetteville, AK 72702
501-521-5566

Employment Contact: Marsha Johnson, VP of Administration
Total Employees: 38
Average Entry-Level Hiring: 20
Opportunities: News—Some working experience preferred. Sales—Will train; any working experience in radio is an asset.
Internships: Yes

DICK BROADCASTING CO.
6711 Kingston Pike
Knoxville, TN 37919
615-588-6511

Employment Contact: Bobby Denton, General Manager
Total Employees: 60 this station, 200 at corporation
Average Entry-Level Hiring: 3
Opportunities: Production, Sales, News, etc.—College degree and some work experience required.
Internships: Yes

DUHAMEL BROADCASTING ENTERPRISES
Box 1760
Rapid City, SD 57709
605-342-2000

Employment Contact: Monte Loos, Operations Manager
Total Employees: 85-90, News 14-15
Average Entry-Level Hiring: ?
Opportunities: Reporter—College degree at school of journalism; training in reporting. TV Production—College degree; journalism preferred. Engineering—College degree and experience.
Comments: "Get your education and then find the experience in internships."
Internships: Yes

EMPIRE RADIO PARTNERS LTD.
1430 Balltown Road
Schenectady, NY 12309
518-381-4800

Employment Contact: Buzz Brindel, Programming Manager
Total Employees: ?
Average Entry-Level Hiring: ?
Opportunities: Programming—Internship experience; work at campus radio station; courses in psychology, voice, English and theatre helpful.
Comments: "Looking for reliable, responsible and self-motivated people."
Internships: Yes

EUGENE TELEVISION INC.
Box 1313
Eugene, OR 97401
503-342-4961

Employment Contact: Jim Averill, Production Manager
Total Employees: 24
Average Entry-Level Hiring: 1-2
Opportunities: Production, News (Technical)—At least two years technical background or college degree. News (Journalism)—College degree.
Internships: Yes

EVENING POST PUBLISHING CO.
134 Columbus Street
Charleston, SC 29402
803-577-7111

Employment Contact: Paul Sherry, Personnel Manager
Total Employees: 1,000
Average Entry-Level Hiring: 10
Opportunities: Reporter—Journalism degree and experience in smaller station.
Internships: No

EZ COMMUNICATIONS INC.
10800 Main Street
Fairfax, VA 22030-8003
703-591-1000

Employment Contact: Laura Daniel, Corporate Personnel
Total Employees: 700
Average Entry-Level Hiring: 80-100
Opportunities: Broadcasting—Experience required. Sales—College not necessary.
Comments: "Since the stations do their own hiring, please call the contact and ask for the listing of stations so you can direct your resumes and questions directly."
Internships: Yes

FAIRMONT COMMUNICATIONS CORP.
700 Montgomery Street
San Francisco, CA 94111
415-956-5101

Employment Contact: Ann Brizendine, Assistant Business Manager
Total Employees: ?
Average Entry-Level Hiring: 2-3
Opportunities: News, Journalism—Experience out of school. No other requirements specified.
Internships: Yes

FAMILY LIFE BROADCASTING SYSTEM
Box 35300
Tucson, AZ 85704
602-742-6976

Employment Contact: Doug, Personnel
Total Employees: 100-200

Average Entry-Level Hiring: ?
Opportunities: Broadcasting—College degree preferred but not required; will train.
Internships: No

FAMILY STATIONS INC.
403 McCormick Street
San Leandro, CA 94577
415-632-5385

Employment Contact: Tina Montex, Promotion Director
Total Employees: 15
Average Entry-Level Hiring: 2-3
Opportunities: Entry-level positions require experience. Technical—Degree required. Writing—Some background in journalism.
Internships: No

FAWCETT BROADCASTING LTD.
242 Scott Street—Box 489
Fort Frances, ON P9A 3M8
807-274-5341

Employment Contact: Dani Falk, Copy Department
Total Employees: 11
Average Entry-Level Hiring: 2
Opportunities: News—Radio experience helpful; degree not necessary. Broadcasting—Work experience at school station; radio school helpful.
Comments: "We look for someone with a good voice that can read well."
Internships: No

FEDERATED MEDIA
Box 2500
Elkhart, IN 46515
219-295-2500

Employment Contact: David Hayes, Director of Staff Development
Total Employees: 1,500
Average Entry-Level Hiring: ?
Opportunities: Broadcasting—College degree.
Internships: Yes

FISHER BROADCASTING INC.
100 Fourth Avenue North
Seattle, WA 98109
206-443-4000

Employment Contact: Julie McCann, Human Resources Manager
Total Employees: 300
Average Entry-Level Hiring: 5
Opportunities: Microwave Production Assistant—Graduation from broadcasting school, experience with audio equipment. Receptionist—Strong word processing and writing skills. College degree required for all positions.
Comments: "Internships play a big part in getting a job."
Internships: Yes

FORUM PUBLISHING CO.
Box 2020
Fargo, ND 58107
701-235-7311

Employment Contact: Milton Schroeder, Accounting
Total Employees: 289
Average Entry-Level Hiring: 3-5
Opportunities: News—College graduate; some experience at smaller station.
Internships: No

FULLER-JEFFREY BROADCASTING COMPANIES INC.
1 City Center
Portland, ME 04101
207-774-6364

Employment Contact: Eve Rukins, General Manager
Total Employees: 200
Average Entry-Level Hiring: 1
Opportunities: Programming—College helpful; broadcast experience. Sales—College not required; experience in sales.
Comments: "Looking for positive and enthusiastic people; good opportunity for women."
Internships: Yes

GANNET BROADCASTING
Box 19610, Washington, DC 20036
703-284-6760
Employment Contact: Laura Chatin,
Assistant to VP/Personnel
Total Employees: 10
Average Entry-Level Hiring: 2-3
Opportunities: Production Assistant—
Experience necessary. Secretary, Assistant
News Director—Two years experience in a
smaller market.
Comments: "Can be promoted from
within. We recommend participating in
internships while in college."
Internships: No

GAYLORD BROADCASTING CO.
Box 25125, Oklahoma City, OK 73125
405-232-3311
Employment Contact: Don McMullan,
Manager of Employment & Training
Total Employees: 350
Average Entry-Level Hiring: 30
Opportunities: Production, Editing—
Previous experience desired. Studies in
broadcasting helpful. College degree not
necessary.
Internships: No

GENESIS BROADCASTING
4030 West Braker Lane—Suite 175
Austin, TX 78759
512-345-9300
Employment Contact: Gloria Ratley,
Assistant to General Manager
Total Employees: 40
Average Entry-Level Hiring: Varies
Opportunities: Broadcasting, Sales—
College degree preferred; experience at
school station; broadcasting or marketing
classes.
Internships: Yes

GHB BROADCASTING
1206 Decatur Street
New Orleans, LA 70116
504-525-1776

Total Employees: 10

Average Entry-Level Hiring: ?
Opportunities: Broadcasting—Experience
preferred. Sales—Will train; helps to have
worked in small town radio station.
Announcers—Work in college station
preferred.
Comments: "Also looking for part-time
help."
Internships: No

GMX COMMUNICATIONS INC.
3866 Dickerson Road
Nashville, TN 37207
615-254-1528
Employment Contact: Amy Stubbs,
Personnel
Total Employees: 30
Average Entry-Level Hiring: 4-5
Opportunities: Sales—College degree
helpful; experience is a factor. People with
a high school diploma considered for
some entry-level work.
Internships: No

GOETZ BROADCASTING CORP.
Box 630
Marshfield, WI 54449
715-384-2191
Employment Contact: Sharon Dupee
Total Employees: 30
Average Entry-Level Hiring: 3
Opportunities: Sales—Must be literate and
a hard worker. Announcer—College
degree required; communication skills.
Internships: No

GOODRICH BROADCASTING
3565 29th Street SE
Kentwood, MI 49508
616-949-8760
Employment Contact: Erin Odle
Total Employees: ?
Average Entry-Level Hiring: Varies
Opportunities: Broadcasting—College
degree and experience at college station.
Sales—College degree.
Internships: No

GO RADIO INC.
Box 550
Webster City, IA 50595
515-832-1570
Employment Contact: Glenn Olson, President
Total Employees: 16
Average Entry-Level Hiring: 1 (News)
Opportunities: Broadcasting—Media courses; college degree required. News—Communications preferred.
Comments: "Will hire people part-time so they can gain experience."
Internships: Yes

GRAY COMMUNICATIONS SYSTEMS INC.
Box 3130
Albany, GA 31708
912-883-0154
Employment Contact: Doug Oliver, VP
Total Employees: 72
Average Entry-Level Hiring: 2-3
Opportunities: Journalism—Degree; experience in school a plus. Cameraman—High school diploma.
Internships: Yes

GREAT AMERICAN BROADCASTING
1718 Young Street
Cincinnati, OH 45210
513-763-5500
Employment Contact: Mr. Larson, News Director
Total Employees: ?
Average Entry-Level Hiring: 2-3
Opportunities: News—College degree required; some experience.
Internships: Yes

GREAT EMPIRE BROADCASTING INC.
Box 1402
Wichita, KS 67201
316-838-9141
Employment Contact: Marshall Porter, Business Manager
Total Employees: 65
Average Entry-Level Hiring: 2-5

Opportunities: News—Degree in broadcasting/journalism; or equivalent experience at a college station. Programming—High school diploma, experience and talent.
Internships: Yes

GREATER MEDIA INC.
Box 859
East Brunswick, NJ 08816
908-247-6161
Employment Contact: Lee Kriss, Corporate Office
Total Employees: ?
Average Entry-Level Hiring: 0
Internships: Yes

THE GREEN GROUP
1601 New Road
Linwood, NJ 08221
609-653-1400
Employment Contact: Mary Turner, Receptionist
Total Employees: ?
Average Entry-Level Hiring: ?
Opportunities: Graphics, Photographer—Vocational school. Reporters—College degree in communications. Will train.
Comments: "We consider appearance, distinction and specialized schooling of importance."
Internships: Yes

GUY GANNETT BROADCASTING SERVICES INC.
Box 1731
Portland, ME 04104
207-797-9330
Employment Contact: Wayne Bearor, Business Manager
Total Employees: 100
Average Entry-Level Hiring: 2
Opportunities: Reporter—College graduate required; work experience preferred. Photographer—Skill requirements not specified.
Internships: Yes

HALL COMMUNICATIONS INC.
Cuprak Road
Norwich, CT 06360
203-887-3511
Employment Contact: John London, VP
Total Employees: ?
Average Entry-Level Hiring: Low
Opportunities: On-Air—Two or three years experience. Sales—Degree not required.
Internships: Yes

H & C COMMUNICATIONS INC.
8181 Southwest Freeway
Houston, TX 77074
713-771-4631
Employment Contact: Lisa Cannon
Total Employees: 300
Average Entry-Level Hiring: 1-2
Opportunities: College and experience important for all positions.
Comments: "We recommend working at an independent station for at least a year before applying to headquarters."
Internships: Yes

H & D BROADCAST GROUP
20 Stanford Drive
Farmington, CT 06032
203-678-7800
Employment Contact: Kathy Lengyel, Office Manager
Total Employees: ?
Average Entry-Level Hiring: ?
Opportunities: Broadcasting—College not required. Receptionist—No requirements specified.
Internships: No

HEARST BROADCASTING GROUP
959 Eighth Avenue
New York, NY 10019
212-649-2300
Employment Contact: Maggie McManus, Executive Assistant
Total Employees: 1,300
Average Entry-Level Hiring: ?

Opportunities: Broadcasting—College degree and background experience. Technical—Experience of latest technology preferred.
Comments: "If you are persistent and determined, you will work your way up."
Internships: No

HEDBERG BROADCASTING GROUP
Box 528
Spirit Lake, IA 51360
712-336-5800
Employment Contact: Kelly McCarty, Controller
Total Employees: 15-25 each station
Average Entry-Level Hiring: 1
Opportunities: News, Sales—College degree required. No other requirements specified.
Internships: No

HENRY BROADCASTING
P.O. Box 70002
Fresno, CA 93744
209-266-5800
Employment Contact: Al Smith, VP
Total Employees: ?
Average Entry-Level Hiring: ?
Opportunities: Broadcasting—Experience at a radio station.
Comments: "Send resume and demo tape to program director and we will keep the information on file."
Internships: Yes

HERITAGE MEDIA CORP.
1 Galleria Tower
13355 Noel Road
Suite 1500
Dallas, TX 75240
214-702-7380
Employment Contact: Jack Robinette, President
Total Employees: 650
Average Entry-Level Hiring: 1-3
Opportunities: Broadcasting—A minimum of one to two years experience.

Comments: "Experience could be considered more important in this business than education."
Internships: Yes

HGF MEDIA GROUP

Traylor Hotel
15th & Hamilton Streets
Allentown, PA 18102
215-434-9511

Employment Contact: Karen Smith, Copy Director
Total Employees: 18
Average Entry-Level Hiring: 3-4
Opportunities: Broadcasting—College degree would be an asset; experience at school station helpful. Sales—Internship experience.
Internships: Yes

HICKS BROADCASTING PARTNERS

21 Music Square West
Nashville, TN 37203
615-664-2400

Employment Contact: Barbara Carwood, General Manager
Total Employees: 42
Average Entry-Level Hiring: 5
Opportunities: Sales—College preferred. Programming—No particular background; should work in school.
Comments: "We recommend you work in a small market first."
Internships: Yes

THE HOLT CORPORATIONS

Route 9
Box 34
Winchester, VA 22601
703-662-0123

Employment Contact: Minnetle Strother, Business Manager
Total Employees: 25-30
Average Entry-Level Hiring: ?
Opportunities: All jobs require high school degree and experience.
Internships: Yes

HUMBER VALLEY BROADCASTING CO.

Box 570
Corner Brook, Nfld. A2H 6H5
709-634-3111

Employment Contact: Phil Young, Announcer
Total Employees: 25-30
Average Entry-Level Hiring: ?
Opportunities: Announcing—Some college helpful; experience in school station recommended.
Comments: "You must have a good attitude and be willing to listen and observe."
Internships: No

JACOR COMMUNICATIONS INC.

1300 Central Trust Ctr.—201 E. 5th Street
Cincinnati, OH 45202
404-233-0640

Employment Contact: Eric Seidel, Program Director
Total Employees: ?
Average Entry-Level Hiring: ?
Opportunities: Broadcasting, Production, Sales, etc.—College degree required; courses in business, economics, and marketing recommended.
Internships: Yes

JESUP BROADCASTING CORP.

1250 West Charlton Street
Milledgeville, GA 31061
912-452-0586

Employment Contact: Scott MacLeod, Operations Manager
Total Employees: 10
Average Entry-Level Hiring: ?
Opportunities: News—College degree helpful; experience in college radio station preferred.
Internships: Yes

JOHN WALTON STATIONS

Box 776, Kermit, TX 79745
915-586-3958

Employment Contact: John Walton, President

Total Employees: 100
Average Entry-Level Hiring: 2
Opportunities: All positions—Degree not necessary.
Comments: "Must have a love for the business."
Internships: No

JONES-EASTERN RADIO INC.
1 Carriage Lane—Suite C-100
Charleston, SC 29407
803-571-5555
Employment Contact: Bob Casey, VP of Operations
Total Employees: ?
Average Entry-Level Hiring: 3-4
Opportunities: Programming—Degree not required, but helpful; experience preferred. Board Operators—No requirements specified.
Comments: "Education is needed for managerial positions."
Internships: No

JOYNER COMMUNICATIONS INC.
3100 Smoke Tree Court—Suite 709
Raleigh, NC 27604
919-876-1007
Employment Contact: Dave Weinfeld, General Manager
Total Employees: 23
Average Entry-Level Hiring: ?
Opportunities: Broadcasting—Experience, great voice and delivery; degree not required. News—College degree (journalism major).
Comments: "Must be able to sound professional and read well."
Internships: Yes

KELLY BROADCASTING CO.
3 Television Circle
Sacramento, CA 95814
916-444-7300
Employment Contact: Angelica Vassell, Community Relations Director
Total Employees: 200
Average Entry-Level Hiring: 15

Opportunities: ENG Editor—Internship required. News—Two to three years experience required. Announcers—Three to seven years experience; college not required. Writers—Three years experience. Reporters—Five years experience.
Internships: Yes

KEYMARKET COMMUNICATIONS
2743 Perimeter Parkway
Bldg. 100—Suite 250
Augusta, GA 30909
404-855-0555
Employment Contact: Dawn Calloway, Executive Secretary
Total Employees: ?
Average Entry-Level Hiring: ?
Opportunities: On-Air—College degree not required; talent is the factor. Sales—College degree and experience. Managers—College degree required.
Internships: No

KIMEL BROADCAST GROUP INC.
U.S. Route 7
St. Albans, VT 05478
802-524-2133
Employment Contact: David Kimel, Owner
Total Employees: 25-30
Average Entry-Level Hiring: ?
Opportunities: Announcer, Broadcasting—Degree not necessary; experience at small station or college station preferred. Reporting—Writing/journalism degree; work experience more important.
Comments: "Learn more about a company before you apply there. Your personality should fit the personality of the company."
Internships: No

KNIGHT QUALITY GROUP STATIONS
63 Bay State Road
Boston, MA 02215
603-436-7300
Employment Contact: Jane Marlow, Sales Assistant

Total Employees: 32
Average Entry-Level Hiring: 1
Opportunities: All positions—College degree; communication/broadcasting courses helpful; writing skills; experience in college.
Comments: "We recommend participating in internships."
Internships: Yes

KOPLAR COMMUNICATIONS INC.
4935 Lindell Boulevard
St. Louis, MO 63108
314-367-7211

Employment Contact: Sue Burk, Payroll
Total Employees: 100
Average Entry-Level Hiring: Varies
Opportunities: Broadcasting—College degree required.
Internships: Yes

KULPER STATIONS
399 Garfield SW—Box 1808
Grand Rapids, MI 49501
616-451-9387

Employment Contact: Hazel Van Laan, Head of Accounting
Total Employees: 25-30
Average Entry-Level Hiring: ?
Opportunities: Announcer—College would be an advantage, but not necessary; must have ability to read and have a good sound.
Comments: "Learn to smile while you're talking."
Internships: No

KWTX BROADCASTING CO.
Box 2636
Waco, TX 76702
817-776-1330

Employment Contact: Francis Davis, Accounting
Total Employees: ?
Average Entry-Level Hiring: ?
Opportunities: Anchors, Reporters—College degree required; will train.
Internships: Yes

LEIGHTON ENTERPRISES INC.
Box 1458
St. Cloud, MN 56302
612-251-1450

Employment Contact: Sheila Sandblade, Copywriter
Total Employees: ?
Average Entry-Level Hiring: 2-3
Opportunities: Copywriter—College degree in journalism; experience while in school; will train.
Comments: "Get as much education as possible."
Internships: Yes

L.E.O. BROADCASTING INC.
Box 1776
St. Cloud, MN 56302
612-252-0110

Employment Contact: Maryann Reid, General Manager
Total Employees: 4
Average Entry-Level Hiring: 9
Opportunities: Operator, Shipping Clerk—High school diploma; no other requirements specified.
Internships: Yes

LE SEA BROADCASTING
Box 12
South Bend, IN 46624
219-291-3292

Employment Contact: Ray Slaugur, Payroll Manager
Total Employees: ?
Average Entry-Level Hiring: 30-40
Opportunities: Production—College degree not necessary; experience preferred.
Internships: Yes

LINDER RADIO GROUP
Box 838
Willmar, MN 56201
612-235-1340

Employment Contact: Doug Loy, Manager
Total Employees: ?
Average Entry-Level Hiring: 1-2

Opportunities: Announcing—College degree; some vocational training.
Internships: No

L.M. COMMUNICATIONS INC.
Box 11788, Lexington, KY 40578
606-233-1515

Employment Contact: Pam McCarty
Total Employees: ?
Average Entry-Level Hiring: 4-5
Opportunities: Sales—College degree required; personality. On-Air—Degree not necessary; great voice.
Internships: Yes

LOTUS COMMUNICATIONS CORP.
6777 Hollywood Blvd.
Hollywood, CA 90028
213-461-8225
Employment Contact: Steven Jacobs, Accounting
Total Employees: 50-60
Average Entry-Level Hiring: 5
Opportunities: Programming—College degree preferred. Broadcasting—Work experience required.
Comments: "Looking for personable and enthusiastic people."
Internships: Yes

LOVE BROADCASTING CO.
Box 4596, Biloxi, MS 39535
601-896-1313

Employment Contact: Ms. Stafford, Personnel Director
Total Employees: ?
Average Entry-Level Hiring: ?
Opportunities: Journalism—Degree not required if you have experience. Camerapersons—High school diploma; will train.
Internships: Yes

MAINE RADIO AND TELEVISION CO.
One Congress Square
Portland, ME 04101
207-772-0181

Employment Contact: Maureen Kellam, General Manager

Total Employees: 125
Average Entry-Level Hiring: 5
Opportunities: Production (part-time)—High school or college degree; flexible hours; will train.
Comments: "Must be self-motivated and have some background in broadcasting."
Internships: Yes

MARSH MEDIA
One Broadcast Center
Amarillo, TX 79101
806-373-1787

Employment Contact: Steve Pritchett
Total Employees: ?
Average Entry-Level Hiring: ?
Opportunities: Reporter—Experience from a smaller station. News Photographer—Associate degree; experience preferred.
Comments: "You should work for 6 months to a year in a commercial station to get some experience."
Internships: Yes

MCNAUGHTON STATIONS
208 West Jefferson
Effingham, IL 62401
217-342-4141

Employment Contact: Bob Kralman, Programming Director
Total Employees: ?
Average Entry-Level Hiring: 2-3
Opportunities: Announcing (part-time)—Will hire high school student for weekends. Full-time positions require extensive experience.
Internships: No

MEL WHEELER INC.
21 Country Aire Road
Carterville, IL 62918
618-985-2333

Employment Contact: Steve Wheeler, Manager
Total Employees: ?
Average Entry-Level Hiring: 8-10

Opportunities: News Photographer—
Bachelor's degree with previous experience in school. Reporters—Bachelor's degree. Technician—Technical school experience.
Comments: "The best thing to do is gain experience and work your way up."
Internships: Yes

METROPLEX COMMUNICATIONS
1818 Ohio Savings Plaza
Cleveland, OH 44114
216-861-0100

Employment Contact: Diane Scott,
Administrative Assistant
Total Employees: ?
Average Entry-Level Hiring: ?
Opportunities: General positions—College degree in communications; experience in school station.
Internships: No

MEYER BROADCASTING CO.
Box 1738
Bismarck, ND 58502
701-223-0900

Employment Contact: Cindy Bektold,
Personnel Manager
Total Employees: 275
Average Entry-Level Hiring: 20
Opportunities: Broadcasting, News,
Journalism—College degree required;
experience preferred.
Internships: Yes

**MIAMI VALLEY CHRISTIAN
TELEVISION INC.**
Box 26
Dayton, OH 45401
513-323-0026

Employment Contact: Personnel
Total Employees: 8
Average Entry-Level Hiring: 2-3
Opportunities: Master Central
Operation—High school graduate; prior experience; technical ability.
Internships: No

MID-AMERICA GOSPEL RADIO
One Parkside Plaza—1430 Olive Street
St. Louis, MO 63103
602-254-5001
Employment Contact: Richard Dugan,
Operations Manager
Total Employees: ?
Average Entry-Level Hiring: ?
Opportunities: Board Operator, Announcer—Working knowledge; on-the-job training.
Comments: "Should have the ability to trouble shoot, think quickly and retain information."
Internships: No

MIDWEST COMMUNICATIONS INC.
90 South 11th Street
Minneapolis, MN 55403
612-330-2400
Employment Contact: Priscilla Carlson,
Human Resources Administrator
Total Employees: 200-300
Average Entry-Level Hiring: 2-10
Opportunities: Broadcasting—Experience is essential. Technical people—Must have license.
Internships: Yes

MOFFAT COMMUNICATIONS LIMITED
CKY Building, Polo Park
Winnipeg, MB R3G 0L7
204-774-2461
Employment Contact: Christine Halma,
Administrative Assistant
Total Employees: 500-600
Average Entry-Level Hiring: 10
Opportunities: Broadcasting—Broadcast education and two years work experience.
Production—College degree required.
Internships: Yes

**NATIONAL BROADCASTING
COMPANY (NBC)**
30 Rockefeller Plaza—Suite 1678
New York, NY 10112
212-664-4444

Employment Contact: Employment Office

Total Employees: ?
Average Entry-Level Hiring: ?
Comments: "Even though we are not recruiting externally at the present time, you may send your resume/cover letter to the NBC Employment Office at the above address."
Internships: Yes

NBN BROADCASTING
463 Seventh Avenue
New York, NY 10018
212-714-1000

Employment Contact: Personnel
Total Employees: 25 at headquarters
Average Entry-Level Hiring: ?
Opportunities: Sales (not considered entry-level)—Experience required.
Internships: No

NEWCAP BROADCASTING LTD.
45 Alderney Drive—Box 1007
Dartmouth, NS B2Y 3Z7
902-469-9231

Employment Contact: Beatrice Vanderwal, Executive Assistant
Total Employees: 55
Average Entry-Level Hiring: 3-4
Opportunities: Broadcasting, Production—Appropriate technical training; college not required. Sales, Promotion—College degree required. News Reporter—Bachelor's degree.
Internships: Yes

NEWCITY COMMUNICATIONS INC.
10 Middle Street, Bridgeport, CT 06604
203-333-4800

Employment Contact: Merrie Fedor, Personnel
Total Employees: ?
Average Entry-Level Hiring: ?
Opportunities: News—College degree in journalism. Sales—Marketing degree.
Comments: "Internship experience is very important."
Internships: Yes

NEWFOUNDLAND BROADCASTING CO.
Box 2020
St. John's, Nfld. A1C 5S2
709-722-5015

Employment Contact: Lisa Butt, Secretary
Total Employees: ?
Average Entry-Level Hiring: ?
Opportunities: Reporter, News, Anchor—Certificate from broadcasting school; one year experience.
Internships: No

NEW SOUTH COMMUNICATIONS INC.
Box 5797
Meridian, MS 39302
601-693-2973

Employment Contact: Van Mac, Program Director
Total Employees: 30
Average Entry-Level Hiring: ?
Opportunities: Announcing, News Reporters—College helpful but not necessary; minimum of 6 months experience.
Internships: No

NOALMARK BROADCASTING CORP.
2525 Northwest Avenue
El Dorado, AR 71730
501-863-6126

Employment Contact: Bob Parks, Manager
Total Employees: 13
Average Entry-Level Hiring: 1
Opportunities: Sales, On-Air—High school graduate; reading and writing skills; college not necessary.
Comments: "You should find a part-time job while in school to get experience."
Internships: No

NOBLE BROADCAST GROUP
Box 85690
San Diego, CA 92138
619-291-8510

Employment Contact: Liz Kern, Executive Assistant
Total Employees: 80

Average Entry-Level Hiring: ?
Opportunities: Sales—College degree preferred; internship experience a plus. Production—Internship experience required.
Comments: "Must possess an eagerness to learn."

Internships: Yes

NORTHWESTERN COLLEGE RADIO NETWORK
3003 North Snelling Avenue
St. Paul, MN 55113
612-631-5000

Employment Contact: Wayne Peterson, Station Manager
Total Employees: 16
Average Entry-Level Hiring: 1
Opportunities: Announcer—College degree preferred; minimum of two years of college. No other requirements specified.
Internships: Yes

PACIFIC NORTHWEST BROADCASTING CORP.
Box 1280
Boise, ID 83701
208-336-3670

Employment Contact: Charles Wilson, President
Total Employees: 30
Average Entry-Level Hiring: 10% yearly
Opportunities: News—Experience required; work at school station.
Internships: Yes

PATHONIC NETWORK INC.
1000 Myrand
Ste-Foy, PQ G1V 2W3
418-688-9330

Employment Contact: Celine Potvin, Secretary
Total Employees: ?
Average Entry-Level Hiring: 10-15

Opportunities: Technician—Graduate from technical school. Manuscript Operator, Cameraperson, Programmer—No requirements specified.
Comments: "People often apply at a lower level and work their way up."
Internships: No

PRICE BROADCASTING CO.
434 Bearcat Drive
Salt Lake City, UT 84155
801-485-6700

Employment Contact: Personnel
Total Employees: 40
Average Entry-Level Hiring: ?
Opportunities: News—At least some college; experience at school station while in school. Broadcasting—College required.
Internships: Yes

THE RADIO GROUP
Box 1319
Columbia, LA 71418
318-649-7959

Employment Contact: Miles LaBordet, Operations Manager
Total Employees: 10
Average Entry-Level Hiring: 3+
Opportunities: Broadcasting—Good speaking voice; college preferred; small market radio experience; will provide on-the-job training.
Internships: Yes

RADIO MANAGEMENT ASSOCIATES INC.
175 Derby Street—Suite 41
Hingham, MA 02043
617-749-0858

Employment Contact: Ellen Kalman, Office Manager
Total Employees: 10-15 each station
Average Entry-Level Hiring: ?
Opportunities: Announcer—Degree not necessary; internship experience important.
Internships: No

RADIO STATESBORO INC.
Box 958
Statesboro, GA 30458
912-764-5446

Employment Contact: Michelle Daley, Director of Programming & Production
Total Employees: 12-15
Average Entry-Level Hiring: 5-6
Opportunities: All positions require experience. Sales—College degree required. On-Air—Experience required.
Comments: "Must be willing to work hard."
Internships: Yes

REGIONAL GROUP INC.
38 Fulton SW
Grand Rapids, MI 49503
616-459-4111
Employment Contact: Elsie Ford, Traffic Manager
Total Employees: ?
Average Entry-Level Hiring: ?
Opportunities: On-Air—An internship program is beneficial as well as knowledge of communications.
Internships: Yes

RESEAU DES APPALACHES
C.P. 69
Thetford Mines, PQ G6G 5S3
418-335-7533

Employment Contact: Andree Wright, Personnel Assistant
Total Employees: 50
Average Entry-Level Hiring: 2
Opportunities: Announcer—Courses in announcing; good voice. Journalism—College degree required.
Internships: Yes

THE RESULT RADIO GROUP
Box 767
Winona, MN 55987
507-452-4000
Employment Contact: Pat Papenfuss, Human Resources Director

Total Employees: 27
Average Entry-Level Hiring: 2
Opportunities: Announcer—High school diploma or trade school; part-time college student. News—College degree required. Sales—No requirements specified.
Internships: Yes

ROBERT INGSTAD BROADCAST PROPERTIES
Box 907
Valley City, ND 58072
701-845-1490

Employment Contact: Randy Johnson, Manager
Total Employees: 15
Average Entry-Level Hiring: 1-2
Opportunities: News, Journalism—Two years of college. No other requirements specified.
Comments: "We need air talent for the sports area; call for more information."
Internships: Yes

ROOT COMMUNICATIONS
1100 Blue Lakes North
Twin Falls, ID 88301
208-733-1100

Employment Contact: Karen Lent, Accounting
Total Employees: 48
Average Entry-Level Hiring: 4-5
Opportunities: Each department has specific requirements. Education is very important. News—Send demo tape directly to Doug Maughan.
Comments: "Watch the trade journals for job listings."
Internships: Yes

RSB COMMUNICATIONS INC.
1221 Chapala Street
Santa Barbara, CA 93101
805-962-7800

Employment Contact: Jack Woods, General Manager
Total Employees: ?
Average Entry-Level Hiring: 4-5

Opportunities: Programming—
Broadcasting school or equivalent
experience. Sales—College preferred.
Internships: Yes

SALEM COMMUNICATIONS CORP.
2310 Ponderosa Drive—Suite 29
Camarillo, CA 93010
805-987-0400

Employment Contact: Arnold Brown,
Project Manager
Total Employees: ?
Average Entry-Level Hiring: 1-2
Opportunities: Sales, On-Air, News—
Experience required; the more education
you have, the better.
Internships: No

SHAMROCK BROADCASTING INC.
4444 Lakeside Drive
Burbank, CA 91510
818-845-4444

Employment Contact: Michelle Joanou,
Executive Assistant
Total Employees: ?
Average Entry-Level Hiring: 1-2
Opportunities: Reporters—Accounting
background; college graduate. Secretary—
Word processing skills, Lotus 1,2,3 and
Word Perfect.
Comments: "We like to promote from
within."
Internships: Yes

SORENSON BROADCASTING CORP.
604 North Kiwanis Plaza
Sioux Falls, SD 57104
605-334-1117

Employment Contact: Gaila Schreurs,
Controller
Total Employees: 110
Average Entry-Level Hiring: Varies
Opportunities: Sales, Broadcasting—High
school graduate.
Comments: "It's good to be involved with
the community and know what's going
on in the world."
Internships: Yes

SPARTAN BROADCASTING CO.
Box 1717
Spartanburg, SC 29304
803-576-7777

Employment Contact: Doris Ewell,
Personnel Assistant
Total Employees: 400
Average Entry-Level Hiring: 25
Opportunities: Sales—College degree re-
quired. Production—Some college pre-
ferred; work at stations. News Anchor—
College degree with experience.
Internships: Yes

STAINLESS BROADCASTING CO.
Vestal Parkway East
Bingingham, NY 13902
607-770-4040

Employment Contact: Virginia Jurik,
Office Manager
Total Employees: 50+
Average Entry-Level Hiring: 3-4
Opportunities: Broadcasting—Degree in
communications or journalism required.
Sales—No requirements specified.
Internships: No

STAUFFER COMMUNICATIONS INC.
Box 119
Topeka, KS 66601
913-272-3456

Employment Contact: Libby Reed,
Personnel Director
Total Employees: ?
Average Entry-Level Hiring: ?
Opportunities: Reporter—Journalism
degree; reporting and writing skills.
Internships: Yes

SUBURBAN RADIO GROUP
Box 888
Belmont, NC 28012
704-825-5272

Employment Contact: Mr. Hilker, CEO
Total Employees: ?
Average Entry-Level Hiring: 2

Opportunities: Most positions—Education at a broadcasting school or sufficient courses at a college or trade school.
Internships: No

SUNGROUP INC.
226 Third Avenue North
Nashville, TN 37201
615-254-1070

Employment Contact: Theresa Hammer, Accounting
Total Employees: 8 at this station, 200 in corporation
Average Entry-Level Hiring: 0-5
Opportunities: Sales—Broadcasting or marketing background. On-Air—Experience or background in the record industry.
Internships: Yes

SUSQUEHANNA RADIO CORP.
140 East Market Street
York, PA 17401
717-764-1155

Employment Contact: Joan Spangler, Human Resources
Total Employees: ?
Average Entry-Level Hiring: Depends on need.
Opportunities: Broadcasting, On-Air—Experience at a college or local station; college degree preferred.
Internships: Yes

TELEMEDIA COMMUNICATIONS INC.
1411 Teel Street
Montreal, PQ H3A 1S5
514-845-6291

Employment Contact: Mary Beaudry, Personnel Director
Total Employees: 500
Average Entry-Level Hiring: Under 10%
Opportunities: Sales—College degree and experience preferred. On-Air—Education helpful. No other requirements specified.
Internships: No

TICHENOR MEDIA SYSTEM INC.
100 Crescent Court—Suite 1777
Dallas, TX 75201
214-855-8882

Employment Contact: Maria Hernandez, Personnel
Total Employees: 12 in corporate office
Average Entry-Level Hiring: 2
Opportunities: Announcing—Experience preferred; degree in communications or speech required. Production—Classes or trade school.
Internships: Yes

TIMES MIRROR BROADCASTING
780 Third Avenue—40th Floor
New York, NY 10017
212-418-9600

Employment Contact: Rochelle Evans, Director of Human Resources
Total Employees: ?
Average Entry-Level Hiring: 0
Opportunities: Very few entry-level positions. Positions require extensive experience.
Comments: "We recommend starting in a small market. Internships are important."
Internships: Yes

TRIBUNE BROADCASTING CO.
435 North Michigan Avenue
Chicago, IL 60611
312-222-3333
Employment Contact: Cindy Vivian, Director of Human Resources
Total Employees: ?
Average Entry-Level Hiring: Varies
Opportunities: Not many for entry-level.
Comments: "Get started in the internship program."
Internships: Yes

TSCHUDY COMMUNICATIONS CORP.
15 Campbell Street
Luray, VA 22835
703-743-3000

Employment Contact: Joyce Jenkins, VP of Operations

Total Employees: 15 at each station
Average Entry-Level Hiring: ?
Opportunities: Sales—Will train; college degree not necessary.
Comments: "It is best to get on-hands experience at your school station."
Internships: Yes

UNICOM-UNITED-ROOK BROADCASTING GROUP
Box 8148
Spokane, WA 99203
509-448-1111

Employment Contact: Tery Manley, Human Resources
Total Employees: 25
Average Entry-Level Hiring: 2-3
Opportunities: On-Air—College degree preferred; must have knowledge of technical equipment; computer skills. News—Courses in journalism; creative writing skills.
Internships: Yes

UNITED BROADCASTING CO.
4733 Bethesda Avenue—Suite 808
Bethesda, MD 20814
301-652-7706

Employment Contact: Betsy Peisach, Corporate Relations Director
Total Employees: ?
Average Entry-Level Hiring: ?
Opportunities: On-Air—College beneficial; 2-3 years experience preferred. Put a demo tape together along with your resume. Sales—College degree and work experience preferred.
Comments: "Must be motivated and goal-oriented."
Internships: No

UNITED COMMUNICATIONS CORP.
1570 Lookout Drive
Mankato, MN 56001
507-625-7905

Employment Contact: Sharon Freitug, Business Manager

Total Employees: ?
Average Entry-Level Hiring: 2
Opportunities: News, Technical—College graduate.
Comments: "Should show ability to be in front of a camera and must write well."
Internships: Yes

VERNON H. BAKER STATIONS
Box 889, Blacksburg, VA 24063
703-552-4252
Employment Contact: Mrs. Baker, President
Total Employees: ?
Average Entry-Level Hiring: 1-2
Opportunities: Announcing—Broadcasting school preferred; good voice essential.
Internships: No

VERSTANDING BROADCASTING
Box. 752, Harrisburg, VA 22801
703-434-0331
Employment Contact: David Ridgeway, Vice President
Total Employees: 29
Average Entry-Level Hiring: 4
Opportunities: News—Journalism background and work experience preferred. Engineering—College degree required.
Internships: Yes

VIDEO COMMUNICATIONS AND RADIO INC.
Box 1179
Gillette, WY 82717
307-686-2242

Employment Contact: Michael Berry, Station Director
Total Employees: 18
Average Entry-Level Hiring: 2
Internships: No

WARNER STATIONS
4343 O Street
Lincoln, NB 68510
402-475-4567

Employment Contact: Diana Warner

Total Employees: 30 full-time, 39 part-time
Average Entry-Level Hiring: 1,300-1,400 at all stations
Opportunities: TV Air, Production, Broadcasting—Degree not mandatory, but helpful. Good voice, knowledge of math, good general education and awareness of news events all come in hand.
Comments: "Must be a curious person and be able to see something through."
Internships: Yes

WENDALL MAYES STATIONS
Box 4607
Midland, TX 79704
915-563-0550

Employment Contact: Parker Hanes, General Manager
Total Employees: ?
Average Entry-Level Hiring: ?
Opportunities: Broadcasting, On-Air, Sales—College degree preferred, but not required. Experience is important. Announcers, News—Journalism background and radio experience preferred.
Internships: No

WHEELER BROADCASTING INC.
Box 466
Winona, MN 55987
507-452-4722

Employment Contact: Dee Tingley
Total Employees: 15
Average Entry-Level Hiring: 2
Opportunities: On-Air—License required. Sales—Degree optional; will train.
Comments: "It is important to have internship experience."
Internships: Yes

WILSON COMMUNICATIONS INC.
400 Renaissance Center—Suite 2140
Detroit, MI 48243
313-259-9100

Employment Contact: Dave Olson, Executive VP
Total Employees: ?
Average Entry-Level Hiring: 2-3

Opportunities: Anchor, Production—Previous experience, technical training or degree. Must have good writing ability.
Internships: Yes

WISCONSIN VOICE OF CHRISTIAN YOUTH INC.
3434 West Kilbourn
Milwaukee, WI 53208
414-935-3000

Employment Contact: Vic Elison, VP/General Manager
Total Employees: 35
Average Entry-Level Hiring: ?
Opportunities: Broadcasting—Bachelor's degree; experience while in school.
Internships: Yes

WITHERS BROADCASTING CO.
Box 1508
Mount Vernon, IL 62864
618-242-3500

Employment Contact: Lee Crawford, Human Resources Manager
Total Employees: 20
Average Entry-Level Hiring: ?
Opportunities: Production, News, On-Air, Disc Jockey—Two years of college; equivalent amount of experience.
Comments: "Writing and verbal skills are very important."
Internships: No

WODLINGER BROADCASTING CO.
4350 Shawnee Mission Parkway
Mission, KS 66205
913-384-9900

Employment Contact: Debbie Walsh, Business Manager
Total Employees: ?
Average Entry-Level Hiring: ?
Opportunities: On-Air—Necessary to get experience while going to school. Sales—Degree; some experience; will train.
Internships: No

YOUNG BROADCASTING INC.
3 East 54th Street
New York, NY 10022
212-688-5100
Employment Contact: JoAnn Dimino,
Receptionist
Total Employees: 20
Average Entry-Level Hiring: 2
Opportunities: Sales Assistant, Sales Representative—College degree required; experience in any kind of sales; phone and computer skills.
Internships: No

Section 4

Appendices
&
Index

A

U.S. & Canadian Trade Organizations

**ACADEMY OF TELEVISION
ARTS AND SCIENCES**
3500 West Olive Avenue
Suite 700
Burbank, CA 91505
818-953-7575

**ACTION FOR CHILDREN'S
TELEVISION**
20 University Road
Cambridge, MA 02138
617-876-6620

**ACTORS WORKING FOR
AN ACTORS GUILD**
12842 Hortense Street
Studio City, CA 91604
818-506-6672

ACTORS' EQUITY ASSOCIATION
165 West 46th Street
New York, NY 10036
212-869-8530

**ADVANCED TV SYSTEMS
COMMITTEE**
1771 N Street NW
Washington, DC 20036
202-429-5345

**ADVERTISING CLUB
OF NEW YORK**
155 East 55th Street
Suite 202
New York, NY 10022
212-935-8080

**ALLIANCE OF MOTION
PICTURE AND TELEVISION
PRODUCERS**
14144 Ventura Boulevard
3rd Floor
Sherman Oaks, CA 91423
818-995-3600

**AMERICAN ASSOCIATION
OF ADVERTISING
AGENCIES**
666 Third Avenue
New York, NY 10017
212-682-2500

**AMERICAN ASSOCIATION
OF CABLE TV OWNERS**
100 Peachtree Street
Suite 103
Equitable Building
Atlanta, GA 30303
404-681-0797

AMERICAN CINEMA EDITORS
4416-1/2 Finley Avenue
Los Angeles, CA 90027
213-660-4425

**AMERICAN COLLEGE
OF RADIO MARKETING**
710 Arendell
P.O. Box 1801
Suite 103
Morehead City, NC 28557
919-247-7131

**AMERICAN FEDERATION OF
TELEVISION & RADIO ARTISTS**
260 Madison Avenue
New York, NY 10016
(no phone listed)

AMERICAN FILM AND VIDEO
LaGrande Park, IL 60625
708-482-4000

**AMERICAN RADIO
ASSOCIATION**
26 Journal Square
Suite 1501
Jersey City, NJ 07306
201-795-5536

**AMERICAN SOCIETY
OF TV CAMERAMEN**
P.O. Box 296
Sparkill, NY 10976
914-359-5569

**AMERICAN SPORTSCASTERS
ASSOCIATION**
150 Nassau Street
New York, NY 10038
212-227-8080

**AMERICAN VIDEO
ASSOCIATION**
557 East Juanita—#3
Mesa, AZ 85204
602-892-8553

**AMERICAN WOMEN
IN RADIO AND
TELEVISION**
1101 Connecticut Avenue NW
Suite 700
Washington, DC 20036
202-429-5102

**ARMED FORCES BROADCASTERS
ASSOCIATION**
P.O. Box 12013
Arlington, VA 22209
609-924-3600

**ASSOCIATED ACTORS AND
ARTISTES OF AMERICA**
165 West 46th Street
New York, NY 10036
212-869-0358

**ASSOCIATED PRESS
BROADCASTERS**
1825 K Street NW
Suite 615
Washington, DC 20006
202-955-7243

**ASSOCIATION FOR BROADCAST
ENGINEERING STANDARDS**
2000 M Street NW—Suite 600
Washington, DC 20036
202-331-0606

**ASSOCIATION OF BLACK
MOTION PICTURE AND
TELEVISION PRODUCERS**
6515 Sunset Blvd.—Suite 206
Los Angeles, CA 90028
(no phone listed)

**ASSOCIATION OF CANADIAN
FILM AND TELEVISION PRODUCERS**
700 Bay Street—Suite 1800
Toronto, ON M5G 1Z6
416-598-4587

**ASSOCIATION OF INDEPENDENT
COMMERCIAL PRODUCERS**
34-12 36th Street
Astoria, NY 11126
718-392-2427

**ASSOCIATION OF INDEPENDENT
TELEVISION STATIONS**
1200 18th Street NW—Suite 502
Washington, DC 20036
202-887-1970

**BROADCAST CREDIT
ASSOCIATION**
701 Lee Street
Suite 1030
Des Plaines, IL 60016
312-827-9330

BROADCAST DESIGNERS ASSOCIATION
251 Kearny Street—Suite 602
San Francisco, CA 94108
415-788-2324

BROADCAST EDUCATION ASSOCIATION
1771 N Street NW
Washington, DC 20036
202-429-5355

BROADCAST FINANCIAL MANAGEMENT ASSOCIATION
701 Lee Street
Suite 1010
Des Plaines, IL 60016
312-296-0200

BROADCAST FOUNDATION OF COLLEGE/UNIVERSITY STUDENTS
89 Longview Road
Port Washington, NY 11050
516-883-2897

BROADCAST PROMOTION AND MARKETING EXECUTIVES
402 East Orange Street
Lancaster, PA 17602
717-397-5727

BROADCASTING FOUNDATION OF AMERICA
Box 57
Spencertown, NY 12165
518-392-5590

CABLE ALLIANCE FOR EDUCATION
1900 Beauregard Street
Suite 108
Alexandria, VA 22311
703-845-1400

CABLE TELEVISION ADMINISTRATION AND MARKETING SOCIETY
635 Slaters Lane
Alexandria, VA 22209
703-276-0881

CABLETELEVISION ADVERTISING BUREAU
757 Third Avenue
New York, NY 10017
212-751-7770

CABLE TELEVISION INFORMATION CENTER
1500 North Beauregard Street
Suite 205
Alexandria, VA 22311
703-845-1705

CABLE TELEVISION PUBLIC AFFAIRS ASSOCIATION
1525 Wilson Boulevard
Suite 550
Rosslyn, VA 22209
703-276-0881

CANADIAN CABLE TELEVISION ASSOCIATION
85 Albert Street—Suite 400
Ottawa, ON K1P 6A4
613-232-2631

CAUCUS FOR PRODUCERS, WRITERS AND DIRECTORS
760 North La Cienega Blvd.
Los Angeles, CA 90069
213-652-0222

CENTER FOR COMMUNICATION
570 Lexington Avenue
New York, NY 10022
212-836-3050

CHILDREN'S FILM AND TELEVISION CENTER OF AMERICA
850 West 34th Street
University of Southern California
Los Angeles, CA 90089
213-743-8632

CHILDREN'S TELEVISION WORKSHOP
One Lincoln Plaza
New York, NY 10023
212-595-3456

CLEAR CHANNEL BROADCASTING SERVICE
1776 K Street NW—Suite 1100
Washington, DC 20006
202-429-7020

COMMUNITY ANTENNA TELEVISION ASSOCIATION
3977 Chain Bridge Road
Box 1005
Fairfax, VA 22030
703-691-8875

**CORPORATION FOR PUBLIC
BROADCASTING**
1111 16th Street NW
Washington, DC 20036
202-955-5100

COSTUME DESIGNERS GUILD
7805 Sunset Boulevard
Suite 206
Hollywood, CA 90046
213-876-1667

**COUNTRY RADIO
BROADCASTERS**
50 Music Square West
#604
Nashville, TN 37203
615-329-4487

**CREATIVE AUDIO AND MUSIC
ELECTRONICS ORGANIZATION**
17 Clara Road
Farmingham, MA 01701
617-877-6459

DIRECTORS GUILD OF AMERICA
7950 Sunset Boulevard
Hollywood, CA 90046
213-656-1220

**EDUCATIONAL BROADCASTING
CORPORATION**
356 West 58th Street
New York, NY 10019
212-560-2000

**ELECTRONIC MEDIA
RATING COUNCIL**
420 Lexington Avenue
New York, NY 10017
212-687-7733

**FRIENDS OF NATIONAL
PUBLIC RADIO**
1108 East Capitol Street NE
Washington, DC 20002
202-466-4210

**HOLLYWOOD RADIO AND
TELEVISION SOCIETY**
5315 Laurel Canyon Boulevard
Suite 202
North Hollywood, CA 91607
818-769-4313

**INSTITUTE OF ELECTRICAL AND
ELECTRONICS ENGINEERS**
345 East 47th Street
New York, NY 10017
212-705-7900

**INTERCOLLEGIATE BROADCASTING
SYSTEM**
Box 592
Vails Gate, NY 12584
914-565-6710

**INTERNATIONAL COUNCIL-
NATIONAL ACADEMY OF
TELEVISION ARTS AND SCIENCES**
509 Madison Avenue
New York, NY 10022
212-308-7540

**INTERNATIONAL DOCUMENTARY
ASSOCIATION**
8489 West Third Street—Suite 80
Los Angeles, CA 90048
213-655-7089

**INTERNATIONAL RADIO AND
ELEVISION SOCIETY**
420 Lexington Avenue
New York, NY 10170
212-867-6650

**INTERNATIONAL SOCIETY
OF VIDEOGRAPHERS**
c/o Amer. Society of TV Cameramen
Washington Street—Box 296
Sparkill, NY 10976
914-359-5569

**INTERNATIONAL TELEVISION
ASSOCIATION**
6311 North O'Connor Road, LB 51
Irving, TX 75039
214-869-1112

**MAKE-UP ARTISTS AND
HAIR STYLISTS**
11519 Chandler Blvd.
North Hollywood, CA 91601
213-877-2776

**MEDIA ACTION RESEARCH
CENTER**
475 Riverside Drive—Suite 1370
New York, NY 10115
212-865-6690

MOTION PICTURE AND TELEVISION
CREDIT ASSOCIATION
1653 Beverly Blvd.
Los Angeles, CA 90026
213-250-8278

NATIONAL ACADEMY
OF TELEVISION
ARTS AND SCIENCES
110 West 57th Street
New York, NY 10019
212-586-8424

NATIONAL ASSOCIATION BROADCAST
EMPLOYEES AND TECHNICIANS
7101 Wisconsin Avenue—Suite 800
Bethesda, MD 20814
301-657-8420

NATIONAL ASSOCIATION
FOR BETTER BROADCASTING
7918 Naylor Avenue
Los Angeles, CA 90045
213-641-4903

NATIONAL ASSOCIATION OF
BLACK OWNED BROADCASTERS
1730 M Street NW—Room 412
Washington, DC 20036
202-463-8970

NATIONAL ASSOCIATION
OF BROADCASTERS
1771 N Street NW
Washington, DC 20036
202-429-5300

NATIONAL ASSOCIATION OF
PUBLIC TELEVISION STATIONS
1350 Connecticut Avenue NW
Suite 200
Washington, DC 20036
202-887-1700

NATIONAL ASSOCIATION OF
STATE RADIO NETWORKS
10800 Bainbridge Drive
Little Rock, AR 72212
501-225-6017

NATIONAL BLACK
PROGRAMMING CONSORTIUM
929 Harrison Avenue—Suite 104
Columbus, OH 43215
614-299-5355

NATIONAL BROADCAST
EDITORIAL ASSOCIATION
6223 Executive Blvd.
Rockville, MD 20852
301-468-3959

NATIONAL CABLE TELEVISION
ASSOCIATION
1724 Massachusetts Avenue NW
Washington, DC 20036
202-775-3550

NATIONAL CABLE TELEVISION
INSTITUTE
P.O. Box 27277
Denver, CO 80227
303-761-8554

NATIONAL COUNCIL FOR
FAMILIES AND TELEVISION
3801 Barham Boulevard
Suite 300
Los Angeles, CA 90068
213-876-5959

NATIONAL FEDERATION OF
COMMUNITY BROADCASTERS
1314 14th Street NW
Washington, DC 20005
202-797-8911

NATIONAL FEDERATION
OF LOCAL CABLE
PROGRAMMERS
P.O. Box 27290
Washington, DC 20038-7290
202-829-7186

NATIONAL FRIENDS OF PUBLIC
BROADCASTING
3315 Hidden Hills Drive
Brookfield, WI 53005
414-781-3326

NATIONAL PUBLIC RADIO
2025 M Street NW
Washington, DC 20036
202-822-2000

NATIONAL TELEMEDIA
COUNCIL
120 East Wilson
Madison, WI 53703
608-257-7712

NATIONAL TRANSLATOR ASSOCIATION
Box 628
Riverton, WY 82501
307-856-3322

NATPE INTERNATIONAL
10100 Santa Monica Boulevard
Suite 300
Los Angeles, CA 90067
213-282-8801

NORTH AMERICAN NATIONAL BROADCASTERS ASSOCIATION
1500 Bronson Avenue
Ottawa, ON K1G 3J5
613-738-6553

PRODUCERS GUILD OF AMERICA
400 South Beverly Drive
Room 211
Beverly Hills, CA 90212
213-557-0807

PROFESSIONAL FILM AND VIDEO EQUIPMENT ASSOCIATION
P.O. Box 9546
Silver Spring, MD 20906
301-460-8084

PUBLIC INTEREST VIDEO NETWORK
2309 18th Street NW
Washington, DC 20009
202-797-8997

PUBLIC TELECOMMUNICATIONS FINANCIAL MANAGEMENT ASSOCIATION
P.O. Box 50008
Columbia, SC 29250
803-799-5517

RADIO ADVERTISING BUREAU
304 Park Avenue South
New York, NY 10010
212-254-4800

RADIO AND TELEVISION RESEARCH COUNCIL
15 East 40th Street
New York, NY 10016
212-532-5733

RADIO CLUB OF AMERICA
324 South Third Avenue—#2
Highland Park, NJ 08904
201-246-7271

RADIO-TELEVISION CORRESPONDENTS ASSOCIATION
U.S. Capitol
Room S-325
Washington, DC 20510
202-224-6421

RADIO-TELEVISION NEWS DIRECTORS ASSOCIATION
1717 K Street NW
Suite 615
Washington, DC 20006
202-659-6510

SCREEN ACTORS GUILD
7065 Hollywood Blvd.
Hollywood, CA 90028
213-465-4600

SCREEN EXTRAS GUILD
3629 Cahuenga Blvd. West
Los Angeles, CA 90068
213-851-4301

SET DESIGNERS AND MODEL MAKERS
7715 Sunset Boulevard
Suite 210
Los Angeles, CA 90046
213-876-2010

SOCIETY OF BROADCAST ENGINEERS
7002 Graham Road
Suite 118
Indianapolis, IN 46220
317-842-0836

SOCIETY OF CABLE TELEVISION ENGINEERS
669 Exton Commons
Exton, PA 19341
215-363-6888

SOCIETY OF MOTION PICTURE AND TELEVISION ART DIRECTORS
14724 Ventura Blvd.—Penthouse
Sherman Oaks, CA 91403
818-905-0599

**SOCIETY OF MOTION PICTURE
AND TELEVISION ENGINEERS**
595 West Hartsdale Avenue
White Plains, NY 10607
914-761-1100

**STATION REPRESENTATIVES
ASSOCIATION**
230 Park Avenue
New York, NY 10169
212-687-2484

STEADICAM OPERATORS
108 Church Street
Philadelphia, PA 19106
215-CALL-CAM

**TELECOMMUNICATIONS RESEARCH
AND ACTION CENTER**
P.O. Box 12038
Washington, DC 20005
202-462-2520

TELEVISION CRITICS ASSOCIATION
332 State Street
Schenectady, NY 12301
518-374-4141

TELEVISION INFORMATION OFFICE
745 Fifth Avenue
New York, NY 10151
212-759-6800

TELEVISION OPERATORS CAUCUS
1730 M Street NW—Suite 407
Washington, DC 20036
202-296-2233

TV BUREAU OF ADVERTISING
477 Madison Avenue
New York, NY 10022
212-486-1111

U.S.A. FOUNDATION
214 Massachusetts Ave. NE
Suite 240
Washington, DC 20002
(no phone listed)

**UNITED NATIONS
CORRESPONDENTS ASSOCIATION**
Press Sect.—Room C-314
U.N. Secretariat
New York, NY 10017
212-963-7611

UNITED PRESS INTERNATIONAL
1400 I Street NW
Washington, DC 20005
202-898-8000

WALTER KAITZ FOUNDATION
660 13th Street—Suite 200
Oakland, CA 94612
415-451-9000

**WHITE HOUSE CORRESPONDENTS'
ASSOCIATION**
1067 National Press Building
Washington, DC 20045
202-737-2934

**WOMEN IN BROADCAST
TECHNOLOGY**
2435 Spaulding Street
Berkeley, CA 94703
415-642-1311

WOMEN IN CABLE
500 N. Michigan Avenue
Suite 1400
Chicago, IL 60611
312-661-1700

**WRITERS GUILD
OF AMERICA, EAST**
555 West 57th Street
New York, NY 10019
212-245-6180

**WRITERS GUILD
OF AMERICA, WEST**
8955 Beverly Blvd.
West Hollywood, CA 90048
213-550-1000

**YOUNG BLACK
PROGRAMMERS COALITION**
P.O. Box 11243
Jackson, MS 39213
601-634-5775

ℬ

U.S. & Canadian
Trade Publications

ADVERTISING AGE
Crain Communications, Inc.
740 North Rush Street
Chicago, IL 60611
312-649-5200

ADWEEK
5757 Wilshire Blvd.
Suite M110
Los Angeles, CA 9003
213-937-4330

or...

49 East 21st Street
11th Floor
New York, NY 10010
212-529-5500

AUDIOVIDEO INTERNATIONAL
Dempa Publications Inc.
400 Madison Avenue
New York, NY 10017
212-752-3003

AUDIOVISUAL COMMUNICATIONS
PTN Publishing Company
210 Crossways Park Drive
Woodbury, NY 11797
516-496-8000

AV VIDEO
Montage Publishing
25550 Hawthorne Blvd.
Suite 314
Torrance, CA 90505
213-373-9993

**BACK STAGE/
SHOOT**
BPI Communications Inc.
330 West 42nd Street
16th Floor
New York, NY 10036
212-947-0020

BILLBOARD
Billboard Publications
1515 Broadway
39th Floor
New York, NY 10036
212-536-5002

**BME'S TELEVISION
ENGINEERING**
ACT III Publishing
401 Park Avenue South
New York, NY 10016
212-545-5100

**BROADCAST
ENGINEERING**
Intertec Publishing
9221 Quivira Road
Shawnee Mission, KS 66215
913-888-4664

**BROADCAST ENGINEERING'S
EQUIPMENT REFERENCE
MANUAL**
Intertec Publishing
9221 Quivira Road
Shawnee Mission, KS 66215
913-888-4664

BROADCASTING
Broadcasting Publications Inc.
1705 DeSales Street NW
Washington, DC 20036
202-659-2340

**BROADCASTING CABLE
YEARBOOK**
Broadcasting Publications Inc.
1705 DeSales Street NW
Washington, DC 20036
202-659-2340

BUSINESS RADIO
National Association
of Business & Educational
Radio
1501 Duke Street
Alexandria, VA 22314
703-739-0300

BUYING GROUP NEWS
13490 Prospector Court
Victorville, CA 92392
619-241-2514

**CABLE & STATION
COVERAGE ATLAS**
Warren Publishing Inc.
2115 Ward Court NW
Washington, DC 20037
202-872-9200

CABLE MARKETING
Jobson Publishing Corporation
352 Park Avenue South
New York, NY 10010
212-685-4848

CABLE TV BUSINESS
Cardiff Publishing Company
6300 South Syracuse Way
Suite 650
Englewood, CO 80111
303-220-0600

CABLE WORLD
1905 Sherman Street
Suite 1000
Denver, CO 80203
303-837-0900

CABLEVISION MAGAZINE
Diversified Publishing
Group
825 Seventh Avenue
New York, NY 10019
212-887-8400

CED
Fairchild Publications
600 South Cherry Street
Suite 400
Denver, CO 80222
303-393-7449

CES DAILY NEWS
Hampton International
Communications
211 East 43rd Street
New York, NY 10017
212-682-7320

CES TRADE NEWS DAILY
Communication Channels Inc.
6255 Barfield Road
Atlanta, GA 30328
404-256-9800

CHANNELS
Act III Publishing
Television Group
401 Park Avenue South
New York, NY 10016
212-545-5100

COLLEGE BROADCASTER
National Association
of College Broadcasters
Brown University
Box 1955
Providence, RI 02912
401-863-2225

COMMUNICATIONS
Cardiff Publishing Company Publication
6300 South Syracuse Way
Suite 650
Englewood, CO 80111
303-220-0600

COMMUNICATIONS TECHNOLOGY
Transmedia Partners, CT.
Publications Divisions
50 South Steele Street
Suite 500
Denver, CO 80209
303-355-2101

COMPUTER PICTURES
25550 Hawthone Blvd.
Suite 314
Torrance, CA 90505
213-373-9993

CORPORATE TELEVISION
P.S.N. Publication
2 Park Avenue—Room 1820
New York, NY 10016
212-779-1919

CORPORATE VIDEO DECISIONS
Act III Publishing, Technical Group
401 Park Avenue South
New York, NY 10016
212-545-5100

CREATIVE NEW JERSEY
P.O. Box 327
Ramsey, NJ 07446
201-670-8688

CURRENT
Current Publishing Committee
2311 18th Street NW
Washington, DC 20009
202-265-8310

DAILY VARIETY
5700 Wilshire Blvd.
Suite 120
Los Angeles, CA 90036
213-857-6600

DEALERSCOPE MERCHANDISING
North American Publishing Company
401 North Broad Street
Philadelphia, PA 19108
215-238-5300

ELECTRONIC MEDIA
Crain Communications Inc.
740 North Rush Street
Chicago, IL 60611
312-649-5200

**ELECTRONIC SERVICING
& TECHNOLOGY**
CQ Communications
76 North Broadway
Hicksville, NY 11801
516-681-2922

EMMY
Academy of Television Arts
& Sciences
3500 West Olive Avenue
Suite 700
Burbank, CA 91505
818-953-7575

FACES INTERNATIONAL
G.S.G. Publishing Inc.
9255 Sunset Blvd.—Suite 210
Los Angeles, CA 90069
213-463-2237

FILM/TAPE WORLD
P.O. Box 6639
San Mateo, CA 94403
415-571-7210

THE 4TH MEDIA JOURNAL
Virgo Publishing Inc.
13402 North Scottsdale Road
No. B-185
Scottsdale, AZ 85254
602-483-0014

THE HOLLYWOOD REPORTER
The Hollywood Reporter Inc.
6715 Sunset Blvd.
Hollywood, CA 90028
213-464-7411

IN MOTION
In Motion Publishing Company
1203 West Street
Annapolis, MD 21401
301-269-0605

INSTALLATION NEWS
Bobit Publishing Company
2512 Artesia Blvd.
Redondo Beach, CA 90278
213-376-8788

**JOURNAL OF THE AUDIO
ENGINEERING SOCIETY**
Audio Engineering Society Inc.
60 East 42nd Street
New York, NY 10165
212-661-2355

**LOCATION PRODUCTION
GUIDE**
P.O. Box 617024
Orlando, FL 32861-7024
407-295-1094

THE LPTV REPORT
Kompas/Biel & Associates Inc.
P.O. Box 25510
5235 North 124th Street
Milwaukee, WI 53225-0510
414-781-0188

MARKEE
HJK Publications, Inc.
1018 Rosetta Drive
Deltona, FL 32725
407-574-6358

**MEDIA INDEX
PUBLISHING**
P.O. Box 24365
Seattle, WA 98124-0365
206-382-9220

MILLIMETER
Penton Publishing
1100 Superior Avenue
Cleveland, OH 44112
216-696-7000

MIX
Act III Publishing Inc.
6400 Hollis Street—#12
Emeryville, CA 94608
415-653-3307

**MOTION PICTURE, TV AND
THEATRE DIRECTORY**
MPE Publications Inc.
Tarrytown, NY 10591
212-245-0969

MSO
TransMedia Partners
50 South Steele Street
Suite 500
Denver, CO 80209
303-355-2101

MULTICHANNEL NEWS
Fairchild Publications
7 East 12th Street
New York, NY 10003
212-741-6700

NATPE PROGRAMMER
NATPE International
520 Stokes Road
Ironstone Building B-11
Medford, NJ 08055
609-654-1830

**OFFICIAL VIDEO
DIRECTORY
& BUYER'S GUIDE**
Palm Springs Media Inc.
P.O. Box 2740
Palm Springs, CA 92263
619-322-3050

**PERFORMANCE
MAGAZINE**
1203 Lake Street
Suite 200
Fort Worth, TX 76102
817-338-9444

POST
Post Pro Publishing
25 Willowdale Avenue
Port Washington, NY 11050
516-767-2500

**PRIVATE CABLE
MAGAZINE**
National Satelite Publishing Inc.
P.O. Box 1460
1909 Avenue G
Rosenberg, TX 77471
713-342-9826

PRO SOUND NEWS
P.S.N. Publications Inc.
2 Park Avenue—18th Floor
New York, NY 10016
212-213-3444

**PROFESSIONAL
ELECTRONICS**
National Electronics Sales
& Service Dealers Assoc.
2708 West Berry Street
Fort Worth, TX 76109
817-921-9062

**PROFESSIONAL
ELECTRONICS YEARBOOK**
National Electronics Sales
& Service Dealers Assoc.
2708 West Berry Street
Fort Worth, TX 76109
817-921-9062

REP
Intertec Publishing
9221 Quivira Road
Shawnee Mission, KS 66215
913-888-4664

RADIO & RECORDS
Radio & Records Inc.
1930 Century Park West
5th Floor
Los Angeles, CA 90067
213-553-4330

RADIO ONLY
Inside Radio Inc.
1930 East Marlton Pike
Suite S-93
Cherry Hill, NJ 08003
609-424-6800

RADIO WORLD
Industrial Marketing Advisory
Services Inc.
5827 Columbia Pike
Suite 310
Falls Church, VA 22041
703-998-7600

RADIO-ELECTRONICS
Gernsback Publications Inc.
500-B Bi-Country Blvd.
Farmingdale, NY 11735
516-293-3000

RELIGIOUS BROADCASTING
National Religious Broadcasters
299 Webro Road
Suite 250
Parsippany, NJ 07054
201-428-5400

RTNDA COMMUNICATOR
Radio-Television News
Directors Association
1717 K Street NWSuite 615
Washington, DC 20006
202-659-6510

SATELLITE BUSINESS NEWS
1050 17th Street NW
Washington, DC 20036
(no phone listed)

SCREEN
720 North Wabash Avenue
Chicago, IL 60611
312-664-5236

SMPTE JOURNAL
Society of Motion Picture
& Television Engineers
595 West Hartsdale Avenue
White Plains, NY 10607
914-761-1100

SOUND COMMUNICATIONS
Sound & Communications
Publishing Inc.
25 Willowdale Avenue
Port Washington, NY 11050
516-767-2500

SOUND MANAGEMENT
Radio Advertising Bureau
304 Park Avenue South
New York, NY 10010
212-254-4800

**STUDIO SOUND & BROADCAST
ENGINEERING**
Link House
Dingwall Avenue
Surrey, Croydon, England CR9 2TA
441-686-2599

**TELEVISION BUSINESS
INTERNATIONAL**
Act III Publishing
401 Park Avenue South
New York, NY 10016
212-545-5100

**TELEVISION & CABLE
FACTBOOK**
2115 Ward Court NW
Washington, DC 20037
202-872-9200

TELEVISION BROADCAST
P.S.N. Publications Inc.
2 Park Avenue—Suite 1820
New York, NY 10016-5601
212-779-1919

THEATRE CRAFTS
P.O. Box 470
Mt. Morris, IL 61054
(no phone listed)

TV TECHNOLOGY
Industrial Marketing
Advisory Services Inc.
5827 Columbia Píke—Suite 310
Falls Church, VA 22041
703-998-7600

VARIETY
Cahners Publication
475 Park Avenue South
New York, NY 10016
212-779-1100

VIDEO BUSINESS
Diversified Publishing Group
825 Seventh Avenue
New York, NY 10019
212-887-8400

VIDEOGRAPHY
50 West 23rd Street
New York, NY 10010-5292
(no phone listed)

VIDEO SYSTEMS
P.O. Box 12947
Overland Park, KS 66212
913-888-4664

VIEW
View Communications Corp.
49 East 21st Street—6th Floor
New York, NY 10010
212-673-7000

WORLD BROADCAST NEWS
Act III Publication
401 Park Avenue South
New York, NY 10016
212-545-5100

Index

RADIO & TELEVISION
Career Directory

The Career Press

America's Premiere Publisher of books on:

- Career & Job Search Advice
- Education
- Business "How-To"
- Financial "How-To"
- Study Skills
- Careers in Advertising, Book Publishing, Magazines, Newspapers, Marketing & Sales, Public Relations, Business & Finance, the Travel Industry and much, much more.
- Internships

If you liked this book, please write and tell us!

And if you'd like a copy of our FREE catalog of nearly 100 of the best career books available, please call us (Toll-Free) or write!

THE CAREER PRESS
180 Fifth Ave.,
PO Box 34
Hawthorne, NJ 07507
(Toll-Free) 1-800-CAREER-1 (U. S. only)
201-427-0229
FAX: 201-427-2037